Free Verse Editions
Edited by Jon Thompson

GHOST LETTERS

Baba Badji

Parlor Press
Anderson, South Carolina
www.parlorpress.com

Parlor Press LLC, Anderson, South Carolina, 29621

Printed in the United States of America
S A N: 2 5 4 - 8 8 7 9

Library of Congress Cataloging-in-Publication Data on File

978-1-64317-196-8 (paperback)
978-1-64317-197-5 (pdf)
978-1-64317-198-2 (ePub)

1 2 3 4 5

Cover art by Aurélia Zahedi.
Book design by David Blakesley.

Parlor Press, LLC is an independent publisher of scholarly and
trade titles in print and multimedia formats. This book is available
in paperback and ebook formats from Parlor Press on the World
Wide Web at http://www.parlorpress.com or through online and
brick-and-mortar bookstores. For submission information or to
find out about Parlor Press publications, write to Parlor Press,
3015 Brackenberry Drive, Anderson, South Carolina, 29621, or
email editor@parlorpress.com.

Contents

v

Contents

Ghost Letters

I

Dear Momma,

Uncle Omar Mouhamed Cheikh said, "Shame. Shame. Shame. Shame and self-contempt. Nausea for me. Nausea for me. We have a Senegalese history teacher." She said, even a black death cannot interrupt the idea of violence. It cannot be erased by any name, it is restrained when it is killed with measure in summer. *Bilay wallah* by any verse, by any *Surah*. These days one of the best places to swim is Sunday at church. Friday. 2 p.m. at the mosque. The sacred places are closed. But we have *Sūrat al Balad* and *Sūrat al Falaq*. We are running out of holy water. May the dead return with their gifts. Beckon to witness what is left of Us. The dead and their conviction. Coded with courage. A clear-cut wisdom. Black death is therefore in Us. *Bilay wallah* slave death is therefore still in Us. It can't blow in the streets of America & France. It can't puff in the summer, May, June, July & August. *Bilay wallah*, it can't even wisp on earth. The *mukhtâr* said, we have Jesus & Momma.

Bilay wallah, the *mukhtâr* & the Pope said. Glory be with Us. Glory be with the Lord. Glory be with Ghost Momma. Black and ghostly are therefore named in sacred songs. Songs of songs. The holy & *Sūrat al Fātihah*. Someone else has dressed it to reduce it. They want to trick it in foolishness. They have fooled it. *Bilay wallah*, they have hustled it. *Esprit colonialiste* ! They bundled it in fear and anger. They have caged it in being black & restrained at high sea & restrained on earth. *Bilay wallah*, Jesus exists. *Bougeureub* exists in *Casamance*. Metamorphosis exists. Dying a black death exists. Farewell exists. Africa exists. Martinique exists. Atlanta exists. Chicago exists. Detroit exists. New Orleans exists. Harlem exists. Senegal exists. Haiti exists. Jesus & France & America & the slaves. *Oradour-sur-Glane exists. Mère Fantôme. C'était le 10 juin 1944.* The Rabbi exists. Departure exists. Baobab & savannah on our backs. We have Senegalese nurses. They wanted departure at the borders. Wanting for peace. We have gone Ghost Mother with Jesus's Cross. We have gone Ghost Mother. We have gone. We have gone. Jesus blessed Us. Forced exiled exists. Momma's songs & prayer in the church. *Bilay wallah* it was exiled by choice to win the war. Momma said, we praised the Lord in the cassava garden.

Dear Mariama,

Ghost Mother said, today is April 4,1968. Jesus came ill & eager to bless Us. He came with mud. It is said Jesus's Tooth ached. It is said you are the nurse who came for songs & a prayer. The village was shut. It is said Jesus knew. You said, Milkman died. Because of his wounds. There was no proof that this was the case. My fears are always candid. The strange way I learned it. Was emancipating. *Je ne rêve pas. Je veux traduire mes rêves. D'un monde mystique.* From the nun. *Suma tour ak suma khél ak jeekeen baléeh.* His mistress. Widow of loneliness troubles my song. *Les lumières veuves.* I kneel at her foot, divine as a God's son & speak to her warmly. I feel her solitude. Milkman has no family. I read to him after his day's work. *On se gonflait. Butées dans les nuits de serments.* He prefers Koranic verses: *Al-Jinn.* Who knew poetry put him to sleep? Let dusk trap this father at his first move of love. Over there, near the village shrine. Is a sacred place where. Mud becomes dangerously ambiguous. When Jesus preached to orphans and termites. Milkman's son Yara Sané walked in his dreams. Uncle Omar Mouhamed Cheikh has a price on his head. I forget his memories. One of his creatures has died, a churchgoer perhaps. *Ô Seigneur a déposé milles fleurs pour soutenir une prière.* Pastors rinse their feet before entering Milkman's chamber. In his verandah, images in mud, and on walls offend evening visitors. *Encore la virginité d'un parfum.* I don't remember why they came to dance for love. I think they came for tolerance & warmth. But how I admire mothers humming as they pass borders in fine virtue. Leaving neither passports nor shadows for *le Raciste* to track them. Elders restore names of the dead. The departed have died a black death. I disguise myself in the mango tree. To wait for owls. Yes, I camouflage myself over wet stones in a form of ache. Immigrants and I wait at the entrance for a church bell. Sharing cold cassava soup and red meat. *Comme des jeunes bienheureux.* I traumatized myself to escape in steam like a ripening vine flowering in *Fleuve Casamance.* Before we meet for *Bougeureub.* I tell orphans to warm a mango soup and find moon. *Écho de mon faible coeur.* To recall complete failure of crusaders. *Fermes ton bec. Esprit colonialiste.* We drip palm oil in our pots. To decorate our bones and hide our secrets in a village mosque. Waiting for Ghost Mother…

these evenings' deluge
darkens our bodies
unhooks & snuffs our courage
owls destruct mango trees   my African skin creates moist mud
and timber
detoxicating mud   severe and cold
I hang myself in fences   (no, I mean on the mango tree)
to avoid   *bonnet*   *du roi sans amour*   *son*   *bateau jaillira*
pour l'Afrique
noir et lyrique
pays natal   *je suis un vautour muet*
mon ombre aveugle se vête
en grand boubou Sénégalaise   *Je suis le fils du défunt*
ghosts and freezing rain

caking up to death   throwing
myself in traps   imagine Milkman tender
bitterly timid
richly human   grieving for Momma   Ghost Momma cries…
"What does it mean for a black boy to fly, to dream of flying and transcending?"
I spoke for numerous   and   distinctive   castes
I rested.

Grandma's Timber Jug

We have gone fragile as a spider's foot.   Don't let Us die out.
Without Ghost Mothers. We drown in a daring & nebulous deluge.

How pleasant to see our hearts puff with the melancholic?
We slog up a stranger's fear over Us, inch by inch, on flagged earth.

From a habit, a good habit to clutch our nightmares.
Très bien. Une histoire. Quitte l'Afrique. Esprit colonialiste !

Bilay wallah, it is said *Allah* thought about the jug. Mango leaf.
Kankourang mask. Hut sketched in cassava leaves. Palm oil & mud.

A jug' stubborn borders, its black, silver, an identity of wounds.
I remember only what my grandmother Nanafall said of a jug,

Nanafall's wishes, that she never wants to be fed through tubes,
That she is afraid to be pierced with a needle by a nurse from America,

Who knows not to speak *Wolof*? Exile stung our raw and distant hearts.
Who wants to join me to wash Nanafall's soul? It would be fitting in

Heaven to reclaim her mulatto of foreign birth body and her restraint ghost?
Wounds droop over my tongue watery pink. Senegalese green. American grace.

First, my grandma's timber jug became part of a routine nightmare.
A trauma of a seafarer's endurance. A slave's blood. Burned black.

Cultures hidden in my palm. Exile bleeding in my body. In Senegal for a visit,
My mouthful of bees, thick in doubt, I pull in front of Nanafall's verandah.

Tormented and stuck in her timber chair, she waves her prayer beads.
She feeds owls, ants & vultures. In my American accent, I search origins of her illness.

My grandmother knows how to track our domestic snake & the termites at dusk.
But I am convinced that a hidden illness (not the virus) is eating her away from Us.

Dear Sibeth Nia Fatouma Ndiaye,

I am in Senegal. It is June 1953. Momma's songs & prayer bring rebirth for Americanized violence in the face of the devil. The Herdsman's bamboo baton burned forever. A curse for our village. Forgive me, my childhood, if by mistake I have buried your gift in my fist. *Damaiy déem Senegal.* I recognize nothing from the Coffin Maker's work. Broken tombs in their chaotic and unparallel arrangement. Vultures came for the corpses. Contrived by Ghost Mother. Tools of my childhood are ants, spiders, owls, snakes, skeletons, moon and mud. Hyenas in a hunger of their own trap, the lilac trees are free. This is not to rupture flatness of life in America. Emerged from the worst of my exile. A needle out to draw blood from owl's neck to heal my African's tongue. *Nasaraane bou méy jangeu dafa doy seuck?* What did I learn in Koranic Schools? Perfume worries me when I scorch memories. I wear it broken to carbonize that evening's ghost. *Ma mère. Sa gloire dans l'ombre du ciel.* Shopkeeper's skirt wrapped over her hips. Disturbed by a thick wind. I open my heart and let trouble guide me to freedom's gates. She looks like Ghost Mother who makes me laugh. That face. Her Senegalese hair. Those eyes. I wink at her. You said, I must suck poor blood from my desolate childhood. You said, I am not innocent. We greet Ghost Mother politely in *Wolof.* Trapped behind cold air that had remained in her skirt for years. Atmosphere in the graveyard is gentle. *Ô Dieu bénit la famille.* A shadow has come to live with me. Sharing a letter that frames three domains: exile, bleeding sun, and blood of my childhood. On Friday, a mother's heart will be carved on a bridge. The village entrance, what could I have written for my dreadful childhood. Blue as snake's bite, I am afraid to look at the village Coffin Maker. Though, the odd obscurity of his work, his work was scenic to watch. How he stabs wood. The pile of wood in his shop. *Le puit du village.* Playing the device of my youth is not difficult after all. Coffin Maker's smell thickened dawn's plants; they stopped flowering. Before uncle Omar Mouhamed Cheikh quit his work, he must talk to his new customer. One-armed schoolgirl fell in the village well. Coffin Maker's work is pleasing even as it ripens. Aunt Jemima said, they will burn his shop, his wish. I am ready to flower in mud. *Très bien. Une histoire. La belle. La bête. Très bien. Quitte l'Afrique. Esprit colonialiste.* Then Aunt Jemima said, we came for Jesus & the elegance

                                        of blackness / a distant
                            Ghost Mother catechized
            indefinite forms of blood
            cemented in a verandah
to privilege   *au cœur de l'Élysée*
                    to claim hyenas' bones as souvenirs
                    although
                    thick heat in Senegal
La Bible. Un vœu. Une histoire. Émotion folle. La belle. La bête.
                                        mask owls as sick girls shift
            through a decade of illness
            their innocent feeling
la République des fantômes   pulling back from history
            to shelter the self
            bruised
            to death
            I am unable to weep   behind my African plot
just humming aches
pledge though to a village shrine / vines and their robust roots lock
                                                    old truth
            from the new kind.

Family Photograph

In Senegal, eleven years are elements of absence from a cassava garden.
Family photograph sleeps under—black in blue—torpid light.
Memories include smiles. They creep in savage vanished years.
J'étais bien incapable de voir ma misère en fragment tendu.

Smiles are brief and cheerful. Regions in faces expose belonging.
My effort is destabilized; I was there still in the photograph.
I see worries, incomplete, but it's possible that before bed, I
Dream of a boy in white kaftan, circumcised & dying in sludge.

Mother looks sunny and young. Mother is black and brave.
I break my vow to ask her, why I left Senegal? Who is Coffin Maker?
In a midst of a terrible grief. Snapped jawbones. Destroyed blood cells.
I fall. Our neglected weeping must be practiced in segregation.

Mother's skin. Mother's face years later. Looking at dust.
Bilay wallah, in her blue headscarf, my grandmother Nanafall is isolated.
Her ghost cracks, it must have been there. Framed in secrets of her own.
I am lost. Because her holy face masks a frightening silence.

That I might barely begin to wrestle Jesus in the mud.
Crawling like a bedbug in grief under Koranic school's blankets.
To suck the mean blood of my childhood. *Hamdoulilah.*
Going back to Senegal. *Hamdoulilah.* In search of exile of my own.

I come close to dressing like a circumcised Senegalese boy.
Father has stolen my compass of dreams. *Hamdoulilah.*
Father has stolen the characters of my youth. *Hamdoulilah.*
Father has not stolen the tongue of my youth. *Hamdoulilah.*

Beating me dead before I cross borders to a land of the free.
I look serious. I am secretly racialized. I am cold in the photo.
Mother lingers on the right, underneath her face,
I cannot explain. There is no hymn, *just pain and history, history, history.*

Dear Fernanda Mbelezi Mabenze,

Village's watch repair shop flooded in Saint Louis (*N'dar* in 1865). A bone in the bridge of my throat is permanently out of place. It lives after years and years of exile. *Bunta safara lay dém ak sama basang.* Wanting to drown in a toolbox among ruins in the Muslim graveyard. I do not like to have my picture taken. Down by a gate that opens to Hell. Policing the shop. Kerosene lamp in hand. His neck thick and ready to strike like a scorpion in the cassava garden. Instead, he licks my wounds. His poisonous sting undoes a watch—when he laments—how hard it is to fix. He rings a watch like a dead bell. *L'école buisson-nière.* He doesn't know that I hid my secrets in his watch repair shop. You and your secrets, too. A Jesus's Cross. You are a lover. You and Yara caressed angles. Elders of all elders, what grows poor in his poor heart, flowers and breakdown at night. For the past months, I have been visiting Yara. His delight over a life of poverty. *Maman osera chanter.* A doctor has filled his anger with dirt. His lungs full of dust, now he doesn't bleed or make a sound. Now he chews cola-nuts. Builds himself. His proper kaftan. A kaftan uncle Omar Mouhamed Cheikh custom-made for Milkman's birthday. Milkman never said he was in pain. He feeds on his own loneliness. His ghost wakes our nature of solitude. His ghost hugs our planet of orphans. Coffin Maker said, it is too soon to settle for happiness. Officer X refused to work in good faith. Destroying my pride in the American way. Killing me before that other Americanized violence. Mas-samba, the Shrine Keeper said, it is so soon to recover from our sorrow. Imam said, but it is necessary to find sources of courage if we want to move on. His ghost dehydrates our nightmares. This father is openly a believer. *Dama beu-gueu ndéki ak askane bï sene yarkar tass.* Saying good bye overwhelms me, Ghost Momma said, today is December 5, 1955.

> grief is a meaningful grace
>
> light a village   Ghost Mother gave me a jug of milk
> where everyone has died of hunger
> *Africanness*
> a ghost is aware of me
> thrill of dying *Vénus. Ma douleur symbolique.*
> youth ripening to fracture, tedium of a generation
> we wonder
> sorrow of
> our bright childhood   *Fermes ton bec. Esprit raciste. Ton bruit de tonnerre. Esprit colonialiste.*
> dealing through

Ghost Momma & Jesus said:
        "there is no pleasant wisdom in Americanness"
but there are... Monsters. Guns. Violence. Mud. Sex. Passports.
Whiteness. Lies. Arrival. Dust & the telling of "Tales"
                    displacement, one nation
                                        under strangers
over some kind of God
                        the Ghost of violence
                                            brutality
                        hidden immigrant mothers
                                        their boys
            offering homage
                    a broken tongue
                                drumming restless
worries in *Xalam* and *Tama*.

Ghost Mother Return for Jesus

Le Christ aux sabots fendus, Ghost Momma says, *avec Ses symboles.*

Hear me dear prophet, Ghost Mother arrived bleeding.
I wear her aches & worries around my body. Jesus's Mouth gone dead.
For our imagined crime, our splendor going against Nature—

Where we planted drawings of our tribe—in that other world
My vague African tongue, blood that is mixed and filthy.
I am unable to snap the door of exile and instead, I lick

Flowers budding in the American way. At the door of no return in clusters.
I have nothing but Ghost Mothers and a thick accent resembling a baobab trunk.
I have nothing, but a thick accent. Its western beat. A Rabbi's *Challah* bread. The blessing.

Unbroken and pure in Jesus's Water, *l'araignée de l'Océan Atlantique.*
Alone in my Senegalese law of faith, I hid with the gods in white garments.
For a *goût de grâce*, I want holy *Bissap* from the prophet's chamber

To numb my tender body and my mouthful of hooks. Jesus's filling Tooth aches.
Months later, alone in the chamber, unable to curve my tongue for Muhammad's dialect,
The walls open and close at night when Ghost Mother returns harmless and brave.

"Boy, forget about Washington and remember your passport number," she said.

Dear Aliyah Awa,

Coffin Maker called villagers underneath the baobab tree. Telling them it is Sunday, March 21, 1965. Walking with Jesus. The nurses. The midwives. Aunt Jemima & her devices for praising the Lord. The *Diolas* are used for this new tongue. The *Diolas* are invited to emerge. They came with sacred wood & mint leaves from the cassava garden. *Bilay wallah,* the *Diolas* emerged from long borders. It was 1960. *Je suis le fils du défunt.* To emerge black and blue alone. *La boue. Du sang. Être noir n'est pas un crime. Mon sang dans ta violence.* I have all kinds of fear to tell you, Aliyah Awa. Fear of neglecting my prayers. Fear of snagging a bus for Sunday's Mess. Fear of catching a bus to soccer practice. Fear of catching a bus for SAT test. *Ces souvenirs.* In my chest, a biblical ghost and a Koranic verse are perspiring in glamor. Breathing unseen memories. Kneeling for unknown beasts not in my country of birth. A new culture hangs firmly. But out of sight. I overhear a shower of applause from mango leaves. *Jaam nga fanan khamo lou sama mame guiss.* I feel welcome in America where English is now useful. Isolation and nostalgia fracture. Bodies bend & break in blue forms. Even when my black skin remembers wounds & the snake changes her night dress. Her fluid force and her landscape are places I know. I find my way to a village mosque without asking Ghost Mother to roll-down windows. I notice air hissing soft prayers through dust & Yara has mistaken me for milkman's visit. Yara's father (The Milkman) came to see him this morning. Ripped out of everything, I would weep for my broken childhood. Split of my youth. Uncle Omar Mouhamed Cheikh cries for a different kind of courage. To be something in my skin. Avenues festooned carefully with qualities of other women (Senegalese, French & American). I hug Milkman tenderly and I shall see him in a dream. The beautiful and delicate matter for our correspondence. Misguided by a form of writing, but I know how to walk over a puddle of salt, even if poisonous. I am ready to worship dead hours, for that, I thank you. There would be another form of life, after the short-lived, I hope to give you back not only the rest of my life, but the kerosene lamp and the black scarf. *Gnoune gneup ay badolé légnou gnon gnii kii ni di beukeu dée ak hiifeu.* Forgive me. Forgive me. Forgive me. These letters are knotted with my new tongue. I am writing in this new tongue. *Un serpent était derrière la clôture. Se régaler de fines feuilles de mon enfance.* How is it possible? How is it possible?

Le Seigneur!   Ghost Mother gave me butter & red meat for the church
        refugees have been sick, they were traumatized at the border
    bodies shaken in front of children   a revolt I don't know
                        what's left to be destroyed
                        a little boy stripped of his childhood
                        wishing I were your shadow
            prayer distracting beauty
            to shutting
            of our worst pride
            exile and darkness stabbing
our tongues   how am I to recover
            have you salvaged ghosted candles?
            Ghost Mother, send language & Jesus
            they say everything
            I must learn how to trace owls and vultures to feed them
                            I must know how to dress like their
                feathers
I must know how to make a book of poems, the Koran & Bible forever in the Nile
                                    rewriting
        for a new bloodied tongue   American ghosts.

Beaten Tongue

I

A boy's childhood tears hang in salt water.
Remember an assault in a Bronx home.

I know about being a stranger & a part of me wanted to sing
Unloved songs, like a growing lost boy eating a fried pot-of-lice for supper.

I crack open moon & she reveals a tender yolk—before a wish—
Thumbnails puncture my lungs. I have forgotten that I was in the jungle.

II

A voice soft—spoken and suggestive—they say:
But maybe a hint of hunger and a new hymn for owls and my new tongue.
Stiff in each note to wake burned black bodies in hidden pits.

How much better do I need to sound?
How much do I have to share?

I finally summoned courage to stand up,
And / just like that / the beehive waved off / turned to:
Soggy mud, owl, ghost, Milkman, Coffin Maker & aches.

III

I am trying to recover from stings poisoning my tongue.
I am trying to recover from a disease whitening my black skin.
Where I came from, what I left behind, a worry I won't voice.

A broken slate I found in a dustbin is sinking in charm.
A small hand stitched cotton purse under Ghost Mother's pillow guards my secrets.
Peaux des serpents. Démasquées. Pour guérir les malades. Les flous. Le Mal.

In every dream, I am deluged with reminders,
Heaven is where freedom & safety bud.
America is not my land. Anyway, maybe America is my home.

Dear Yu Yan,

It is said, "one Togolese student was unable to find a place to stay when he was evicted." You said I must kiss a Jesus's Cross. It is said, "University shut down campus housing." Ah, I forget, "he took to sleeping under a bridge until he was chased away by police." What kind of angel must I kiss? You said, "Blue LED screens have formed small portals into violence, beauty, tragedy, and nonsense." Of course. My God! It is said, "a Nigerian student was given just hours to evacuate his" home. You said to kiss an angel dying a black death. *El Dorado—damalén jéppii.* Kerosene lamps failed when Imam called off the gods. That day, there was a Koranic recital at dusk. I need a voice. I need *Sūrat al Balad* and *Sūrat al Falaq* and a new dream. Being chocked from static aches. Here aches are being emptied from a body. *Meuneulogno touss deeygney bëett seey frontiéere.* I know who I have been. *Abaal ma ghén yayboy deumeuyii damalén diakhaal.*

I read the shadow of the Pope in French & in Wolof. Jesus's Letters in the church. Jesus's Milk from the village shrine. Mud and voodoo in me. It is said, we are dying. It is said, "fruit stands, clothes racks, and suitcases spill into" Jesus's Roads. Aunt Jemima & the shopkeepers are no longer selling candles. Beggars wailed all night keeping me awake. Snakes do not cure nightmares or my illness. It is said, "a Muslim Chinese woman" is braving Jesus. It is said, "an African man in a long, sand-toned kaftan" is loved by his exile. He loves the smell of *Yassa.* I keep voices in my ears. *Ndax dégg nga Americain?* I wish for a cry of owls, their horrendous silence. Their grace, a speck of evil I might embrace. Their hunger for wet mud I envied. Their colorless skin mourns for breeze it knows. Barbets caring rice farms ask to share rice I receive from a village orphanage. Wishing these birds farewell is a hard task. It is said, "black men in loose, silk shirts, right behind them" is Ghost Mother's sweat. How I used to adore their whistling. Singing in summer dawns. *Maman je t'embrasse très fort. L'amour. M*ère *fantôme repoussez tes bras.* In my ethnic village, a tune bangs voices coming from mosque & church. *Ndax dégg nga nasarran.* In my native village, a *Kora's* tune bangs rebel's gunfire. It is a loner's sound. It is said, priests are "waiting for their fish." Ah, I almost forgot their frozen feathers. Warmth it hooks in my poor black heart. Before I cross the sea, I smell your lovely skirt. It is said, they "sectioned-off sidewalks." It is said, "sidewalks were barred to Africans." *Quand*

l'esprit Sénégalaise farandole. Mother clutching her children, they are afraid of the sea. To drown slowly, I wait for growing sun & hide devil in my tongue. Uncle Omar Mouhamed Cheikh bargained your skirt for schoolgirls begging for water. To dissolve dust bridging lost and wounds in their throats. They need blankets...
do not marry the president   I say... to her marry the Milkman

Ghost Mother is not gutting

vessels landscape   hallows open fields

our nightmares blowout

a passage   letting our raw

wounds take flight for the bush

echoes of sniper's bullet

vanish

for a sound we can't read at dawn & in darkness

of infested waves

so distant our youth   each of us curves

time   at the border   the future limits itself to

witness, captive wind   near village shrines

fear braces my mouthful of owl's feathers

the village nurses & midwives came for a peaceful daybreak

safety shimmers for its hidden plan   *Je suis le fils du défunt,*

I walk with Jesus towards Senegal, France, America & China.

Bush Boy's Correspondence

Dear Father: my accent is different they say.
It must be time to search for my absent childhood.
But for the quiver of this poem: let me be silent.
Le Christ avec mon sang précieux sur la croix !

My bruises are almost healed. A tooth is not missing.
The dream comes out again & again & again & again.
It buds in my crushed soul. But I have Jesus's Tooth & Tongue.

I agree with Uncle Omar Mouhamed Cheikh.
Let you & me grow separate.
Let Us keep peace. I look around me & see
A mother. She tenders carefully & I feel safe.

The way I carry this new land. I want a life of plants.
Inside me harvest. Flowers of Evil outgrowth in a westernized cassava
Garden. Mango trees. A spirit that bleeds blue blood.
Owls— watch yards free of weeds. I wonder. I wonder.

Dear father: mother knows why owls beat ghostly wings.
Mother knows what caged owl needs. Feels. Wants.
Racines. Le Dieu. Fardeau. Enfer. La neige. La boue. Masque. Miroir. Muse.

What does a safe blanket do? I want to answer.
To our lone companion. My lips crack & dry from the whippings.
I am frightened. I feel so poor. I am so Senegalese.

The pride I lost & never got back.
A Senegalese, black, and dense pride ripens.
Who would believe the story—discreet—
I have not spoken or peeled my melancholic skin. Yet.

Dear Zamira Safiétou Faye,

Ghost Mother said, today is May 25, 2020. *Bilay wallah*, Coffin maker said color of grief is black. Uncle Omar Mouhamed Cheikh said I found a meal, but I am not free. Uncle Omar Mouhamed Cheikh said I must not let daemons prevail. Fences of silence are tearing me down. *La lumière douce des bougies. Rythme facile. Je me respirais pour dormir avec les vautours.* Free me from ruin. Free me from exile. Free me from dead bodies I see in nightmares. *Louy ndéyou talibé booy dem dii yélowan ak yérem you xotékou.* I am rotting as my sable skin is a danger to America. I want to witness Ramadan months. Church's anniversary. Wondering about your psyche. My psyche. Bodies. Psyche of blackness as uncle Omar Mouhamed Cheikh called it. He said, *Bukki di léy deuguë balla guay jaaru ask deumeuyii.* Our worries fire permanent loneliness. Lonely me dies alone. Scribbling thoughts from a frightful mind. I think of illness I have suffered all these years. Nothing matters. But bodies next to me. Flowering at sea. You said to turn to sunken black bodies and Jesus for tenderness. Restrain with what you said. A timber Jesus define despite raw aches. How many ghosts need to know? How many slaves are buried under *their* homes? *Hommage pour chaque rose.* They must want to see a naked black boy in a Jesus's Tunnel. My God! A terrible sin, truly to my sorrow. Boy in tunnel is sick. I am sick and debased by my struggles. Nothing. But. House hold snake is my companion. I visit her in dark hours of the night. I take myself to the village tunnel where death is no stranger to Us. The village Herdsman is exiled. Near the rocky desert. It is said the village breeder is exiled. Uncle Omar Mouhamed Cheikh said. Black death is no stranger to Us. Death is no stranger to a body. Uncle Omar Mouhamed Cheikh said. Mother's death is no stranger to Us. She curls herself in pearls and I hug myself with trapped worries. *Maman votre atmosphère.* To transform our routine. You waited for clouds to disperse. Before I gag my mouth, I use empty jars for drums and make Senegalese music. Inside tunnel, you and I transform our voices into a biblical tune. Before a flood. It is said, Ghost Mother did not like appearing in weddings. I was told, Ghost Mother liked to appear in burials. She let dust dance for the dead and for our tribe's song. Drowning myself in the Mediterranean Sea. In mud. Fairly black. I was mud. I weep once more telling Ghost Mother *Sa fierté…*

mon sang précieux.

my youth

　　　　　　　　how bleak is poverty

how difficult its music

how being black in the world is difficult

　　　　　　　night glows

a blank space

　　　　a lonely space

to ghost　　　　　　　　　the music of mother's heart

　　　　in the tunnel

I am masked

using moist wood and lion skin　　　protecting my skin

I find a welcome

I miss on earth　　what I knew　　I learned when I

learned it in the drowning　　hour gives a blue symbol

　　　　　　　for a body

　　　　　　　for bodies

dusk is kissing vaporized wind

a blind boy's cry

swinging thorough loss

yellow clocks are ticking towards New York City, Paris & Dakar for African masks...

Massamba a Shrine Keeper Is Trapped in Owl's Nest

Shrine Keeper is trapped in a body hanged in baobab. It is not dead.
He was afraid to speak for acacia leaves & the blown up secrets of a shrine.
It is said he caused shame for villagers. Tribes drift with wind digging for them,
Old memories. Villagers' terrors! My God! He begged for his life. He was innocent?
Now, I wonder how to drag every baobab tree to a sacred place.
Cassava garden where I would want to be a witness & speak to Ghost Mother.

Before I swore to my village Shrine Keeper. How to extend my law of faith.
In a garden of last and holy flowers? The camels arrived to carry his body.
He wished to have three lungs. He burned all his crude desires.
It is said that Shrine Keeper buried something under mosques & churchyards.
He warned me that death was coming. Prompt as a braking body.
Prompt as Ramadan month. Prompt as slave death.

Blue nightmares came to finish our history.
Shrine Keeper gone, all I had were my two eyes to cry.
It is said Shrine Keeper survives for long periods
Without food or drink. By using up blood reserves in his swellings.
Arrived to cut branches. Carried bread, in a birdcage.
Witnessed evening sky crystallizes into remains.

Bilay wallah, it is said, uncle Omar Mouhamed Cheikh licked his wounds.

Dear Destiny Kiara Khadija,

Ghost Mother said, you wish to be saved by the church & Jesus. My body split open when Ghost Mother casts her ballots. The coffins & their keepers. *Je suis le fils du défunt.* A village appointment room. I leave and I shall not return except with proper nightmares. You & Aunt Jemima sat home & stayed for my arrival. Worried for my return home. Uncle Omar Mouhamed Cheikh said, he never arrived home on time to save me. *L'écroulement de ma naissance.* They dip their fingers in ink. With oblique meanness. A meanness that would not yield for years. *Fatéwoumala.* Bring bread & groundnuts to workers. They don't know these workers. Blue snake, black bodies, yellow sun, and ghost have been lost. Cruelty from bodies protect Us from day of ruin! I cross borders for my poor blood crumbling in black, blue & red soil. You said I must forgive. Like a new god. *Un ciel décoloré de cristal.* Evil throwing its shadow to snake. We have nothing left. A brute broke my body. A brute broke your heart. *Bougeureub* in deluge, I fall with ghosts. Uncle Omar Mouhamed Cheikh told me I must wait for a flood to travel ahead. *La mort d'un amour.* African faces turned into gods, is a work done by Master Thief. He left me with sick children. Master Thief left me mud. African faces turned into *Art* for a museum is work done by Master Thief. *Le paradis de la nuit.* A village river is poisonous. I color my world in grief. I am not allowed to say words for home. Uncle Omar Mouhamed Cheikh said, he is furious. Foreigners came to the village. They gave Us food for the church & the mosque. They are teaching English, German & French. Instead, foreigners are not teaching: *Wolof, Diola,* & *Bambara.* I am allowed to say words of my skin. Words about my skin. Uncle Omar Mouhamed Cheikh said. Farms are burned black. Fables disappear. A beast unlocked my chest & filled my trunk with Shrine Keeper's spirit. *La joie du travail nouveau.* Blue ghosts shut paradise and hook their prayers in clouds. As I keep sick owls company, I serve them bread and cheese. *Santa sama yayboy.* Not all that strange to think of Ghost Mother, gone forever, gone while I was a boy

unknown

sees secrets

when loneliness and beauty

strike

comfort nothing

ache and complete despair

a hunter's kill
Nat Turner
mystique and afraid of white's devices
Je vais mal à present. Ma douleur symbolique.   my solitary cage cracks
my lonely body cracks
it yields years to free me
over confession
obviousness & gratitude
lingering & turning aside
for   blue   Gods'
sharpening
nouveau laws
trapped in mesh
I can't explain

zeal
of my youth
before I sink with
my dirty blood.

Tapestry in Faith

Bilay wallah, I want to tell you about nights at home in the Bronx.
A family evicted over the aroma of a Senegalese dish, broken

Fading into a ghost, Mother weeps as palm
Oil spreads its lines, in a saucepan. Youssou N'Dour's music was on.

Flamboyant smells linger on halls.
I mean flamboyant African smell lingered.

Months on & on & on.
Mr. Williams, our American landlord nagged
At my stepmother about smells, rent & loud Senegalese music.

My stepmother was pregnant with Salimata,
What seems after all to have been progress.
Our papers almost signed by America.

Is there anything more wonderful
Than vines growing to snakes,
Beside long rivers, owls & vultures
Taking flight to do work at night?

Sitting somewhere public. Maybe in New York City,
I come close to crying out for a Senegal city vista.

Ghost Mother's perfume inside my childhood,
My stepmother abandoned & now so difficult to trace.

If I come from a sacred village, the deaf Shrine Keeper knows my song.
(But Mustapha, our village Herdsman is my hero).
His long black headscarf & his long black bamboo baton are blessings.

Maybe I'll be ready to grieve in Dakar, maybe it is all right to be afraid.
Billay wallah, life in America is a collection of flamingo's graves.

Dear Aline Sitoe Diatta,

It is June 4, 2020, you said, Jesus came for the burial. One girl named Aïssa Maïga is ill & so to heal her. We gave her songs, a prayer & many African masks… Before she is gone from the village. Devices for Nursing Owls have gone dead. Officer X and his Americanized machine. Eating his own nightmares dirty blood & the beast. Ghost Mother said, you are raw, in pain, but vultures came. America knows my despondent body wants peace. *Bilay wallah*, Uncle Omar Mouhamed Cheikh says, look at these tone-deaf birds. Waiting for hushed winds. Waiting to reveal hushed aches from bodies. Uncle Omar Mouhamed Cheikh said. I am faithful as African skins in the Atlantic Sea. You said, Aunt Angela is one of the Ghost Mothers. I am faithful as black bodies in lonely America, *Hamdoulilah. Le fleuve du Sénégal emporte tout. Eau froide.* His fable is hanged in a bare limb of a baobab. *Damay dem Senegal sunu gaal.* We fed black birds on damp & windy days. What happened to him in dreams? Ghost Mother catechizes me & says stay with sunlight so you can die in peace. Uncle Omar Mouhamed Cheikh said, so, you won't die a black death. In a lonely pit with priests, whose wounds he licked for my grace. I hide in mosquedomes to study, the Imam who wants a duet with Ghost Mother. Run for your life from a chimney-shaped cloud before dusk. Thorns and hornets are awake to guard my broken childhood. My body is so ashamed. Our bodies are cleaved of elegance. *Chantent une chanson des rois Sénégalais* ! Ninety (or seventy birds) are in a sky longing for tolerance. In a fading mist, look up: owls guide their lovers inside trunks of baobab's nude body. After *Bougeureub,* uncle Omar Mouhamed Cheikh and his desires. Dancing with Jesus and ghosts. I am not sure. You said I must forgive again. Uncle Omar Mouhamed Cheikh arranged our wooden Koranic boards. *Sougnou Mamboy.* Aunt Angela & I set traps to save girls & good wives at the border. As I put faith in a spider, exile & the Chancellor. I numb my body of its worries. Ghost Mother returns from the farm with a boy in her arms. She sponges him with her black handkerchief. *L'Océan Atlantique grossit rapidement. Je suis le fils du défunt. Ma jeunesse.* Being black & a villager is a good faith. I am not alone in the village shrine. Ghost mother is with me. Inside me, I feel the ache. I dignified myself in a pit with the vultures   the Chancellor came for Us. . . . *Un vice. La justice. Mes racines. Ce peuple.*

to escape smell of the dead & make peace with them
Jesus & the Pope hardly made it   through the border, but Ghost Mother
& Aunt Angela came

Ghost Mother looks after my childhood
fastening logs with a new tongue
a fear I think is alive in owl's nest
masking the African body terrifies me   African masks for every future
of every future   I trade my Senegalese blood
for a snake body
how to bite my new tongue
I learned it in church
I learned it in Koranic school
I learned it in the streets of America
I learned in the streets of Paris   merging ghosts
sweat growing in charm
vacuuming up
what I learned from cassava gardens & the streets of Berlin
my new tongue is too inept to lick moist mud
I rot when mothers and their babies sink in the Atlantic
& turned to stone with Ghost Mother & the *mukhtâr*.

Reliquary

We travel inland in cuffs with bruised up skulls for a credo.
Hooked to robust iron ends and troubling waters in Île de *Gorée*:
Of fear, we are defeated so we freeze our bodies to zero.

Having no idea. Unable to read blood on blown-off flesh
Or, why blue wind—suddenly hates the way we hug peace
To find ourselves within dead villagers—ghosts in the shrine.

We outlive everything in a sanctified place we never kept alive:
Ghosts and owls traded with snakes, timber, sex for kola nuts.
Cassavas sober to black. Bodies died with sunflowers.
L'homme qui vend du café sénégalais montre sa maîtrise.

Designed with infinite patience for the unspoken brutality.
Here, discolored monsters know how to hurt in silence.
We scrub our dark skins counter-clockwise privately,
To make rhythm with our feet for the unspoken violence:
Beugeureub, Kumpo, Kankourang, Tama & Xalam.

Not to heal raw wounds, or disremember history, but to embrace
With chainsaws & axes gutting our new tongues. English dialects.
More than narration; we carried our tribe, *balafon*'s dead gourds.

Dear Hapsatou,

You said, we will not go play near the bodega. The block is hot. Blood, dust, mud & curfews. You said, Momma's songs and prayer lit the jungle so master is confused before we trap him for rebirth. You said, even with a curfew we are nursed with Jesus's Milk. Uncle Omar Mouhamed Cheikh said, *Hamdoulilah*! I was baptized with faithful blankets. He said. I am baptized by heavenly nuns, *Hamdoulilah*! A body's loneliness goes way back. I composed death in a church & mosque. I suffered & crumbled in marvelous ruins. Now I mask my skin in ruined cassava gardens. New chairs in church and mosque are painted black so they won't be visible in darkness. Prayer rugs have plants festooned in them. Flowers from the garden of Eden. Flowers from the Casamance Sea. For the dead. *Lettre à la religieuse aveugle du village.* Flowers from the Dead Sea. *Dans les déserts.* Flowers from the Dead Sea. Flowers from destroyed cities. *Des villes majestueuses.* For the burial of the dead. Who came with their dead, *Hamdoulilah*! Here I am haunted by the tedium of truth. I have built a new blanket for my imagined heaven. Outsiders enter first. They are welcome with figs and cheese. *Au Sénégal, je meurs avec les oiseaux charmeurs.* I am at war & barely welcomed by my new home. A *mukhtâr* speaks to me about womanliness. Life and tolerance. He asks me about forgiveness. I admire the *mukhtar*, his modest soul. A humble soul I seek. Handing guards my passport I panicked like all émigrés seeking smiles from other passengers. Reality of anxiety is still poisoning my body. I couldn't speak a word of English. A guard spoke no *Wolof* or *French*. An irony of seeing a stranger cry for real! I proceeded to a bench assigned to undocumented travelers. Real suffering began when a guard began asking questions. *Le soleil éclairait mon immense désespoir.* For reasons of this poem I must not say a word. Except that my father had never told me I would be questioned before guards allowed either of Us to enter America. A guard looks not in our eyes. A process that makes Us human in a world of boredom. What happened to freedom? *Dougnou ak jam dougnou ak mbam dougnou ack xajjii.* I ask to use a toilet: it was empty & I wrote struggles and exile on walls. Seems to me that beautiful struggles are freedom. Ghost Mother, too, realizes that my isolation goes way back

My childhood has lost   all its meaning
a stolen youth   abandoned a culture   a wife &   children…
Hamdoulilah! Flowers from destroyed cities and the Dead Sea lived on for
                    the dead   (…my mother of course)

            tell me about a woman emptiness
                        faith—for a woman she loved
in her placenta
        mother shielded   blood that controlled her shame and her sadness
                    in her guts— she hid tears just for the dead
    pray for   her ordinary   faith in her placenta   for
burial   in her garden
                            for nine months
bees sting; spirit to suck neatness of the moon   neatness of the fetus
                                        protecting
                                            thunder of our sins
            I let everything in a body break
        I let everything in a body died
                America you have violence; we have *Sūrat al Masad*
                        for peace.

34

Fragment

Bilay wallah, it is not truth
I can't be a jogger,
but a single note,
single talk, one body
bleeding in your machine
making your crimes wrench
therapy and form
From art irrational

What does blackness have
if malice, violence, & horror is all
you are aware of?
Have I escaped being, Senegalese,
African, black and colorful
or faithful to my Jesus? You choose.

What do museums have
if African faces are all
you are aware of—Master Thief,
have I died a black death
on your boulevards? You choose.

Ghost Momma said, "glory in our skin."

Dear Yasmine Yafa Abu-Rabia,

You said, we are the children of God. Momma's songs and prayer lit the streets of Paris. *Ah! Helas! Ce peuple. L'histoire de la France. Mes racines.* So the exiled won't eat mud. You said, we are children born in amazing love. Ghost Momma has guarded me all my life in her cassava garden. Holy rocks and holy flowers. Ghost Momma is guarding Us & the holy plants at the desert. She worries about the nurses at the border. *Je suis le fils du défunt.* Uncle Omar Mouhamed Cheikh said, Ghost Momma is guarding me all my life in her unfailing faith. I am learning how to be me (the blood of my dark skin ripples with unease). What they call a free world does not survive, my uncle said. Whose welcome do we dance for? Jesus asked, what is welcome? Jesus asked, what is violence? I recall uncle Omar Mouhamed Cheikh. In his wet and muddy verandah. His dark blue Kaftan stained with Jesus's Blood. When I was not wanted. Nightmares after me. The blue monster after me. I know about a crime of displacement. Borders are metaphors. Exile is a metaphor. Officer X after me. His Americanized violent machine. *Wallah,* I know about forced exile. Flowers of the Dead Sea. What have I done? What have I done? Mother, death is freedom. *Wallah,* dying a black death is not freedom. Uncle Omar Mouhamed Cheikh said, the color of my skin troubles America. I grew up from time to time. I tried to allow memories blossom in me. Me mother, me I struggle. I have struggled to understand snow-white gods. Bruised and choked by my new faith. The faith of being American, black, & of Jesus, & of *Allah.* I think of boys begging in streets of Senegal. But my father who abandoned everything *just* for America. For 20 years. Father needs a green card. Uncle Omar Mouhamed Cheikh said, Churchgoers praised my father's hunger. Mosquegoers praised his deadly faith. Mud in the American dream. Museumgoers praised his doubtful faith. Being Americanized. Had always been his device for survival. He has starved himself for years. *J'observais un cadavre.* My father lets me soil graves for blessings I do not want. In me—a stubborn baobab of broken leaves. You said Ghost Momma knows about Jesus' secrets, too. The unknown meets my godly skin and peels it artfully. My God, how nifty of America! I am in the cemetery with Lamine the gravedigger & I am ready to follow him. He wants company for his pilgrimage to Hell. Hell is hotter than a free world he says. Dear Yasmine Yafa Abu-Rabia, acacias yielding in graves are budding for our broken dream. Our dangerous and deadly dream. There is that old Senegalese saying. I know a great throne does not make a great king. I know how to camouflage myself in traps (a symbol I stole from the village shrine for Jesus). *Car un cheval tué reviendra.* I recall telling the *Mukhtâr* at the border... in *Wolof*...that... Massamba the Shrine Keeper

                         cried for our suffering   we are the displaced

     our blood   &   our hunger   at the border   formed a

                                             large

                                        wound

                      that grew in a passage of my throat

        it is crowded with visitors   and the dead

        such paths   uproar

old stones   from my uncle's native village

                   and now at midnight

Coffin Maker   &   scholars   &   nomads   bump shoulders

    a sick Senegalese woman   &   a sentimental lover

    sing the name of their bishop   they tug their hair

puzzled by silly life   of   literature and theatre events

Ghost Mother   & shadow of street lamps are not melancholic anymore

          missing the noble village houses   housekeepers

      nurses &   midwives

      don't hover over conservative meals in my native village

             a schoolboy sells

bamboo wood   palm oil &   his hunting   gifts to pay his way   for

lectures on ghosts in jungles and fables of   the Shrine Keeper Massamba

   the pickpockets   &   the dead stare at doctors

&   let sight-seers crawl towards   the clarity of their loneliness

                 in their throats   fear & freedom

sick for years

        alone in my lonely faith & the magnificent scars

                        every day

             they witness sunset leaves tenderly falling

mud   owls   love   blood   the chameleon's secret   air

      water   hoofed

sendoff   kisses

              their blue hearts in Ghost Momma's

       songs and prayers

upgrading a bond of freedom in a body   *Je suis le fils du défunt*
       Bilay wallah

                their bodies

vigorous   with   mercy   but   whiteness
      thinking
     about clandestine
       Ghost Mother said, "they brought Us powdered milk but we don't
have water"
our hunger unwrapped the secret of   whiteness   &   violence & hope
             are locked away   in   a
       shackled   *favela*
somewhere   death   &   starvation   is
         guiding   Jesus   into
      the beautiful   the universal   &   the ugly
         black   American
    African

    Senegalese like me…   *Hamdoulilah*!

Ghost Mother & Papa

African boy runs in her yard.
Sister's voice begins, harsh & curious.
"You ought to be ashamed!"
What has the boy done?

She built a summer house in dreamland.
A humble, a humble home and this too was
A fake, but nothing haunts a summer house.
When I moved in with her, father died,
Lynching himself for a meaning—
What kind of meaning? A meaning for whom?

And if I translate, I might hear Jesus and His chosen people .
How father compromises with saints in bed.
I am unable to explain a form of hunger. A form of discomfort.

We have a disease from haunting nightmares.
Ghost Momma going be a historic Goddess.

History allows me to confess:
J'ai des souvenirs rouges de sang.
Alors. Très bien. Je te défit. Quitte l'Afrique. Quitte l'Afrique.

I must clutch everything from my lost childhood.
Use it carefully. Warned a Nun.
Une dame belle. Bronzée. Malaisée.
Me tue frugalement. Quitte l'Afrique.
Bizarre mort qui partage destinée. Aussi de destinée.

Of her hand, the summer house still hugs
In each melancholic echo,
tick, tock, tick, tock, tick, tock, tick, tock
dribs of black blood; her new lover left behind.

This evening is our last night; at dinner I honor her.
She did not allow me to touch. Touch what. Touch what.

She desires herself in authorized clothes.
Due promptly as a slave death.
She coils & disappears.
I have been waiting for years, for this sacred & long-night,
Where bees only ooze for joy in the cassava garden.
"Boy, forget about John Adams and remember your SSN number," she
said.

Dear Aramata,

Bilay wallah; Ghost Mother postponed her faith to stitch my dream. She weeps: Isn't a body. Isn't a body. Isn't a body. Ghost Mother said, judge my boy he did not do it! The beautiful people cried for Adama. Ghost Mother said, judge my boy he did not do it! Who we are? Who we are? We are imagination. We have imagination. Milkman said. Black flies were vicious last night. But I draw every shadow of Ghost Mother in the sand. Are you watching over Us? Ghost Mother said, judge my boy he did not do it! I walked by cassava gardens and doors of freedom are bolted. Entrances where every symbolic flower of the desert caressed like Ghost Mother. In my wish, I am still holding your hand. *Seynii weexay nii guy boudoul mëgnii.* I need your hands for sacred words. *À pieds joints. Je bois l'eau miraculeuse.* So, after dawn prayers, black birds started to fly in harmony. I thought of reshaping my world without solitude. Solitude is a gift to me. Loneliness is a gift for a body. You know. I remember what you said about how black snake is here to heal my wounds. I have fewer tears now. Mother, my *dorsal raphe nucleus* is rotten. Aramata said he must love Lamine. She has loved Lamine. Aramata & Lamine seek Ghost Mother for prayers. They teach me about womanliness. My *dorsal raphe nucleus* has been blue for years. Mother, tears are healed wounds. We are staying beautiful and may even burn our skin to black. Remember it was burned formerly. See, we burn a body now to build a new beauty. Are black flies here to cure new wounds, too? Milkman's witnessed you horribly bleeding. Milkman's awful timing. Seeing things he was not supposed to see. Drums. Mud. Owls. I have been shackled by history. I have been learning acceptance from you and Lamine. Drums I have made with lion skin. Drums I play to heal my sickness. Here are heals wounds. Not the imagined crime. When Jesus's Tooth is dead. But image of a traveler. That American judge signed out the warrants. Jesus said, to watch out for the devil's burden. We are blessed by the Pope and Ghost Momma. . .

<blockquote>
midnight bending   its neck   to indicate vanity
     lamp bruising black
licking   the
     silhouette
   of my dark skin
unhands me
I have missed church bells on Sunday
</blockquote>

I have missed mosque's calling of   gods
  I camped with Mustapha the village last Herdsman
    I admired   the way he called   the   vultures   in sacred songs
     to survive   Milkman said, "nobody was killed…"
   owls & Ghost Mother

                              sing withdrawn hymns
so I battle   against   my new thinking

from a black belly   from a black fetus
             carefully   sharpening
hooks for a journey   helping / worn

                            who Jesus dresses up
to let black stars kiss *them* American   here   now   what pride
    passports   roots   all in it together?
All that have been disseminated from our history : Reparation. Sins. Slaves.
       yours truly,

Symptom

I consider other ways to earn silence.
Midway through writing a poem,
Ideas already finished, a setting in place,

Each stroke gives me a dozen holy flowers,
From the Dead Sea. Flowers blossomed for late spring.
Flowers. We let them blossom for the welcome

Of crowds from the destroyed cities.
I wear maps of my origin, *Kumpo mask*,
Senegalese, dense black skin. Treasures.

In my heart hangs a slave linked to my genuine solitude.
American now, perhaps, but with a Senegalese ear.
Who I have been; I know, what I have done.

A dark truth, but here, a violent atonement.
The hurt of my childhood, like when my foreignness
Crumbles, & restores itself. Tied as a slave chain.

I disguise my native tongue. A chameleon. I may travel
In pictures, pictures themselves, I pull out
A locked razor. My lyric cry for broken dreams.

Dear Seynabou,

Sympathizers are christened with Jesus & African Timber Owls. Their nocturnal songs. We vocalized our broken dreams from exposed branches. The emptiness of baobab. Coffin Maker walks amongst Us. *Yéesu.* His callused-up hands. *Yéesu.* His callused-up hands are from his work. His callused-up hands are faith from his work. *Soo leinn xamoul boulein whxaa ay waxou votée doo touss doo dara yaafouss.* Bodies are chosen people of God. Nightmares are leaving violence. Gravedigger Lamine is thinking. Holiness and a god I find it hard to learn from. Grandfather's prayer-beats you. Last Friday, I walked streets of Dakar when sun was down. I saw beggars sharing cola nuts and papaya with a mute mendicant. God—there is a quiet terror that her silence brings. I cried when she cried. The streets of Senegal keeping prostitutes safe. Your shack has been burned. *Axëe ack yélefou bagane.* Villagers have burned everything. Villagers took Yara's torn wooden reading chair. Their work is not begging. Their work is meaningful to them. Fruit vendors & flower vendors know. They know about prostitutes. Orphan boy lobbied me to carve a mother's grave and scribe words of time. *J'ai tout senti.* I put flowers. Eucalyptus & black stones on soil. Rain is sinking with everything & we are pinned in our dreams. Devil came to rob the Herdsman. Ghost Momma was there in her home. Ghost Momma killed with a no-knock warrant. My difference from that Americanized violence. A body's dreams have broken down. Owl faces her husband. Telling him to learn that color of violence is not white. *Maison d'Arrêt de Reubeus: chambre 40.* That color of violence is not white. It says: whiteness says, color of violence is black. Coffin Maker & his callused-up hands are from making *Kumpo mask.* The market place is deluged again. Meatman's hope vanished. The bareness of rain ripples & smell of your wet hair. Much like you. I will do as orphan boy told me so. I forget. His isolation is implied. His lonely black body. His isolated body means our lives exist in haunting waves of the Casamance Sea. *Ana sama juge.* My God—he asked for a satire and a tragedy, but no special marks— Momma says, the devil came for mud & bodies ... but Jesus wasn't having it...

> Bush boy is secured   and   restrained out there in the jungle
> taking   courage   away
>   a gift dragging   me out of a   black death   *ana sama juge*
>   *Bilay wallah*   so *they* say
>   I am not ready to be   American
>   *Bilay wallah*   so *they say*

I am not American   *ana sama juge*
a body has   been honored
                    a perfect cry meets a flower from a desert
my last breath
            sinking with bees
                                    Bush boy help me
dust the night that comes with the lost vultures // night
    from my trouble
            self-assured in heaven
    America *Bilay wallah*   I am dying
when a body is killed
                        Is a black body final?
                        ᵤ*ᵤ*ᵤ*ᵤ*ᵤ*ᵤ
                    standard—
my captor is filthy   rich his evil deeds— blow oil & tar around   my
lumpy neck
the masters   are threatened
                the road to American-ness
                        Jesus's Cross American-ness
            American highway.

PROLOGUE TO A GHOST MOTHER'S EXILE NOTE VOLUME I

What happens
to a refugee's dream,
when a girl's dream is broken
and her sister
has gone missing
for months & years?
Does it snap like Freddie's spine
inside the emperor's van,
does it bloom
like ancient rosemary
near the Mississippi River?
Does it snap like George's neck?
Underneath Officer X & his Americanized knee
Pinned between Ghost Mother &
Jesus's Cross against Americanized violence.
It die like a prisoner's spine
in a torture chamber in Senegal,
a holy bridge & then faces,
muzzled in a water bucket of the walls:
Je meurs…je meurs…je meurs, Ghost Mother said.
Owls & vultures witness Officer X nags her,
forcing expired pills
in her broken throat
terminal wounds
flower under the bridge
of her long & rosy tongue.
It is said, sour milk
she used to fight insomnia.
It is said, cracks on the walls
she used as a platform,
clapping, laughing at ghosts & ruined results.
She restrained her pain, though fly & spider
gamble their clear-cut faith
to claim territory for *Kankourang*'s oozing,
a bloody border, in their own isolation.
It is said, our broken dreams sagged

& they are ghostly hanging between white walls
of our gorgeous America,
& for our scented France.
Sang des vautours pour expulser le mal.

Bush Boy's Nationalized Hymn

I made you rich, you bastard. Where is my lawyer?
Come speak to me in the jungle, the least you could do

Is listen to Sandra's terror, Breonna's horror, Abner Louima's shock!
When I drum for your privileged songs in the bush. We lie in mud.

A body split open at midday somewhere in America, it puffs for ghosts,
To walk the planet. It knows dying a slave death: *Abdullahi, Arbery, Amari & Zari.*

It knows about being dark-skinned. Brutalized & lonely in France, Théo Luhaka.
Where is my judge? Liberty, society & fairness. Offering to your rules for Adama.

We know about being black & lonely in that other Americanized violence.
We know about failing in prison & understood fully. The Hanging. The whipping.

"Boy, forget about Jefferson & remember to come home for Jesus is here," Momma said.

Dear Lubnâ,

I masked Massamba the Shrine Keeper in the tunnel. Villagers. Nurses. Owls. Milkman & Uncle Omar Mouhamed Cheikh keep going where violence thickens, *Hamdoulilah*! They keep going where a body's death thickens to ghost. Mango trees in cemetery have all gone milky. *J'ai tout touché*. I am running away from church city & I keep going. *Je suis le fils du défunt*. Exile progresses where the moment of loss ripens. I keep going & hope never to turn back for blessing. Going to a country that removes my kind. It is time to learn the language of my youth. Shrine Keeper keeps me company in church. We play with his wounded toys. We keep our wounded toys in our hearts. Toys masked carefully in blue. So, when we go outside, we leave the toys inside the tunnel. *Maison d'Arrêt de Reubeus: chambre 47*. Otherwise. Otherwise. Otherwise, Jesus knows. Jesus knows what we have buried in the tunnel are not slaves. Shrine Keeper is afraid that villagers will find him. Like me. You are afraid. You confessed to me. That villagers are disgusted by work done for the ruined results. Your lover. His lover. Your husband. The gravedig-ger is hiding under the fired bed of my childhood. You remember how Ghost Mother died. Remember songs Senegalese families sung. A voyage in vessel. *Le Joola* capsized to give Us ghosts. Rice and cow's tongue soup served before a burial. A sanctum to imagine a world where *they* say my race does not belong. I was born where a race violated my skin. Verses rehearsed. They are formed in terror so that when I recite them. I know death is waiting. A black body's menace is not novel. Why did Uncle Omar Mouhamed Cheikh say, "it was so simple"? Forget not to say my prayers. My uncle said, *Yalla teerë lii monme bookognon yellowan guinar saa gaat do darra ak seey toubab yooo ley nekhaal. Fokheul sa gate. Feukheul sa tate do darra*. Before I left the house—I whistle to owls so they protect my spirit. So, I took pride in visiting your grave, and then I remember what you said about how misfortune has no appointment. You were always on trial. *Ana sama juge*. For your husband's sins. Sins of slavery. Sins of whiteness. Sins of language. Sins of narration. In the passage, I create borders for your grave,

crossing the margin

crossing the corridors of the Koranic school

there are wounds

telling moments abroad

to create toxics feathers

I am unable

to kiss Jesus's Cross   given His corrosive Teeth   done at the shrine
protecting myself   after   devil's tongue
Massamba maintaining his daily routine near the rice farms (the shrine)
it is difficult work

     purposes of blackness
     seeking peace—
overripe now   I have   Rabbi's *Challah* bread   given to me   a blessing
    I came to cross borders   I hid my notes   under hot heat.

I am reduced
to big & black
to fit a profile X / says captain Palmer
humble   I hold on to
strength,   but ambiguity *in Americanized machines can't kill Us all*
I hold on to Ghost Momma's sweat & moments of loss
that's all that I have.

In Permanent Exile from The Clock Unreachable Neck

Like this: every morning, I ask where is my judge?
I think, whether the bamboo in the streets of America
Would fracture its ribcage at sea with blue Jesus.
From a colonizer's arrogance. Master Thief. His muddy boots.

Let me tell you. I am a misfit. I have *Kankourang*.
I am on a border crossing with Jesus.
I traveled; I don't know. From where?

Hot volcanic tears, carefully guarded.
Pure enough to drink. Momma said,
So long ago, they healed disease in the streets of France.

Consider pink Senegalese tongues,
That sketched my bones & America's overcast / zenith.
Let me into a silent place, in the streets of France,
Where death would never find me. *Kumpo mask* will.

The clock is ticking & Momma is drying her hair,
She had been sick for years eating
Her thoughts & taking expired capsules.
Her black skin peeling off slowly.
Her beautiful black hair falling painfully.
The neatness of her mind sinking to mud & dust.
She wants to live. That is all she wanted. To live.
It has been difficult to help her sleep at night.

She weeps for a breeze we can't find for her.
She weeps for a black blood we can't dilute.
She weeps for a hot bath: we have no more pure water.

In failure, I am trapped between verandah,
America & xenophobia. A new tongue, English & mud.
Uncle Omar Mouhamed Cheikh called:
His sister, Ghost Mother fainted & is dying.
He whispered in Wolof: time is up;
We must bury Momma in the cassava garden.

Dear Angela Ndioro Coumba,

My strangeness is in the church. You are welcomed in the church and in the mosque. Mustapha is our village Herdsman. Mustapha says, you are afraid to be seen by villagers. You allowed refugees to remain for good. Villagers don't know that you hid them in the tunnel. *Sama teewaay moy dara sën teeway doo dara.* Long dark necks are bending patiently to grieve for you. Long African mouths split open for white teeth. Sustained slave bodies buried in ghostly graves. Healers lineup in the cemetery. In master's cynical & deadly greed. *J'ai tout trouvé.* Ghost Mother, wonderful gifts. Seducing a beautiful body. A shrunken faced orphan girl in a village prefers her left hand. She is the gifted one. I am not. She says, the streets of America are not the streets of Kabul. The streets of America are not the streets of Baghdad. She called the crowd & make them dance to blues & Jazz. My only desire is to woo her. Sing songs of my tribe. My grief is transformed into desire. The *Kumpo* is coming for my journey. While I took it all from Ghost Mother *just* for a journey. Tunnel's gothic charms are significantly formed, and they inspire thoughts about time, love, death & space. You and I have agreed to keep our secrets. *Maison d'Arrêt de Reubeus: chambre 42.* My books are filled with tears. They are not pain I feel. You are suffering from history. You are not sure where to go after this life. Heaven? Hell? Stay on earth? You and Ghost Mother before the end. I am telling Ghost Mother before I sink. Coffin Maker wants me to design my own coffin. He says: metal and nails must come from sacred shackles. He says, my coffin must be clasped by villagers at the shrine. Measurements of a body. He says, wood must come from baobab. I am finding myself. Angela Ndioro Coumba, you fractured yourself in dreams. To keep *Mbalax* & *Tama* in a safe place. I am lost in my performance. At night, I leave Mustapha in the tunnel, so your visits are tight-lipped. I am at peace in the sewage. I hold on to praise the Lord. It reconciles me. Travelers I take with my fellow orphans. Are without history. Maybe we are strangers here. At war with our fathers. We used to *salaam* in the mosque with Mustapha. *Je suis le fils du défunt.* Arranged black & white chairs in church. We used to *share* kola nuts. But now we share stories and blankets. Now mother, we recite Maya, Condé, Tony, & Lucille instead. The Koran & the Bible (of course). One evening—I left this—behind for a lone passenger crossing borders,   she did not forget her Jesus's Cross   I tell her in *Wolof* …

dirt on its wings—

*

vultures   owls   a chameleon   and *Bougeureub, Kumpo*
& Kankourang

* waiting for
a cry of childhood
Désordre. Politique. Hyène. Colonialiste. La crise. La vie. Afrique. Malheur. to beg
for peace
barking at Jesus—   soils & mud from forgotten rivers
give tenderness—   meaning burns our black tongues in the rocky desert
unloose
garments from Ghost Mother
wire themselves with flowers for the dead
for purity   *Yéesu ack Yàlla* blessing Us
the drunks from black stars— in these destroyed cities & sacred concrete
yet still blind
mother darkened white candles before she burned them for Us
to help me see in dark alleys of America
loving the loneliness of your broken body.

Biography of Events

Are like *surahs* my Koranic teach misread when *Kumpo* came.
Are like a lover's claim that white America is not racist.

Where, to write *surahs: Al- Fatihah* & *Al-Nas*
You must weep counterclockwise to catch your gasp.

Where, Massamba the Shrine Keeper says, revenge is not
A vague fragment of blue & dark blood.
But, if Nat Turner could speak for August 1831.

But, perhaps to witness our trauma /
A black body's stress / a black death
But, perhaps to trace the history of race.

And the only way to introduce a
Biography of events, is to stage,

A Nouveau Hamlet, in which
I am an African slave & my penis
is cut unsuccessfully.

Dear Astou,

I write today to wish you a good Mother's Day. If it is a holiday to you. Then a very happy holiday. A Fisherman and a sea in flame. Where was *Yéesu*? Consider a fisherman's simple, faithful & patient labor. I have just discovered bodies in a village river. Fisherman Ousmane tells village fathers what to do with black bodies he found in the river. I was told he settled with villagers. Some of the dead bodies have no heads. Bodies cut up into bits. *Sakhal pééxe aggréseuryii sakhal pééxe deumeuyii sakhal kò khél.* Imagine bodies ascending to heaven. When I don't see uncle at village gathering. I know he's preparing for another voyage. In spite of the fact that his health troubles him. He is wondering what would happen to dead black bodies. Bodies died a slave death. When he—himself—dies. Last Friday, rinsing our feet in the fountain. Fisherman said, "being a matter of shame and personal discomfort, was now a thing for pride and public display." Embarking on this last passage. You begged me to rinse the wooden plank covered with blessings. *Maison d'Arrêt de Reubeus: chambre 17.* So, you can take the water with you on your crossing. My uncle's pregnant wife. Astou is home peeling potatoes. She waits for uncle's return. *J'ai peur d'un serpent qui dort.* She asks the children to spread out a prayer rug. Making sure there are no breadcrumbs (under their Mother and Father prayer rug). After evening hours, village chief & the priest deliver some news that has no meaning for anyone. They hand the children. Portraits. Their father's holy book and his blanket. Telling them (and their Mother as well) to mourn for a sainted father. My uncle was a devotee. You are a believer, too. A faithful lover to my uncle. He has confessed again. Who knew my uncle was a sainted father? He healed a village of its devils. His ghost is here to help Us make peace with dead slaves. Slaves who died a slave death. Now uncle's family keeps aloof. Treating everyone with kindness. Hope. A priest tells a fisherman's family, it is absolutely acceptable to forgive. *Au Sénégal la bonne odeur couvre tout.* Confounded with my faith, I tell fisherman's family… Ghost Momma says the devil be out here killing Us…

tolerance is licking fire
from its distance—

thickening
new-born cries &

African babies   *je suis le fils du défunt*
     in their Jesus's Wisdom
Bilay wallah   consider good deeds for earth   holy mud   in my faith for

cassava garden. *Les boues de mon pays.*
Coffin Maker & Aunt Jemima said.
　　　"there is no pleasant wisdom　in Americanness"
But there is . . . Gates of Hell.　Slaves' relics our tribes and the ghosts.
American shackles. Kneeling for the Lord of Mercy. . . .
　　　　　we consider captain Palmer & a sheriff's report for internal narrative
　　　　　　　　　　　　sun is after
　　　　　　　　nudity　　　　　unholy dirt
　　　　　for the sake of　　pure weeping
　　　　　isolated inhumanly
　　　my kind black body has no place
on earth *they* say
　　　　　America can't you welcome that　　Jesus said
　　　　　　　　ain't no more　slaves to give you...

The Meaning of Restraint Revenge

Revenge is not politics. Revenge is Art.

To be a chunk of *the civilized tribes*, you candidly recalled
Ways your black bodies have been burned long ago.
Yoke of selfhood is a way of accepting a black death.
Appearance. Branded by the fact that you were born.

Revenge is not politics. Revenge is art.

Although not all, in the word privilege,
There is freedom, right? Finally, & even
If you could give everything, our everything.

Revenge is not politics. Revenge is art.

Don't you love history? Holocaust & Slavery.
You create dangerously, to sever the skin.
"I am a big black dude," Officer X said, before he ruptures my privacy.

Revenge is not politics. Revenge is art.

You don't peel ripe mango-skin. You remove the dark bowl
Of your being to numb your body from your worries.
Cassava garden. Vultures cleaning after the dead. A native tongue.
Ah! La conscience de ma race. France n'oubliez pas les 16 de Basse Pointe.

It's too bad America. We like it very much *in here*. We are staying.

Dear Hafsa Binétou,

What you said about my stepmother. But father had never told me. That my black body was a threat to white America. That my black body is a threat to France. What you said. About a culture of violence. For what you said. About America being white. For *them* black America is violence. For *them* I am a boy and I am innocent. For them, I am Senegalese. For me & America: I am black from a block. I was to clean everything. That I was a house boy. That I would eat alone. That at seven o'clock in the morning I was to clean a guest room. *Jokkoo Yallah ak Yéesu ak Kharryii ak Tabaski ak jakarta.* I scrubbed a guest room almost every Friday. *Un souvenir mélancolique s'explique.* It has become my Friday routine, among other apartment duties. Sometimes I was watched performing these duties. It reminded me of workers. Workers in bodies. Like undocumented workers. Midwives. Nurses. Milkman's doctor. Like workers in the hospital in Oussouye. I did not miss a spot. Like workers I polished accurately as if choreographed. Did the guest room have fragile walls? Imagine Jesus protecting you. I needed *Kumpo mask*. I do not remember hearing or noticing winds that came from cracks on the walls. The guest room felt like a size of a *mihrab*. Its bright colors, its shaped calligraphy spelled my hopes. Imagine Imam watching you. *Inquiète, j'ai un portrait lumineux du Sénégal.* Karabane island turned my solitude into a gift again. When le *Joola* capsized. Mood there was bleak. Though I cleaned this room every Friday. But I was not allowed to read or play in such a decent space. I think of church. Nuns told me I am a black African boy. In the tunnel after supper. Before I hiked to the sewage. You then said a black body is a gift. *Maison d'Arrêt de Reubeus: chambre 20.* In the end, as I grew older. I remember the guest room being filled with Ghost Mother's odor. You said, *boy*. Healed the nightmares. Ghost Mother's odor protected me from my father's and my stepmother's terror. It healed my dark skin from aches. When I walk away from a Bronx home… I mumble Koranic verses, for

the Other's language   madness in prison   isolation   then

I hit the block for thieves & beggars … before   deportation

sea betrays time

to let in   a blaze   the one eyed overseer

who flogged villagers   spoke no *Wolof* & *Diola*   so he was

trapped   by vultures & termites in mud

*

pain is opening up *Le village. Malheur.*
I am mud
the agony from all parts of life
shadows dance to blues
shadows dance to jazz
shadows dance to

our tribe songs
our Senegalese rhythm *Mbalax* and *Beugeureub.*
elements of faith
hooked in long black necks
marching for forgiveness
light shares
its peace with
black stars
asking for understanding of blessing in *Wolof* and *Diola*
unhooking what… blood… master… & the devil
I kneeled, too… for Jesus & Momma
to unlock gates of arrival.

Bush Boy's Wooden Slate

There is no distrust in the Holy Wooden Slate.
Is stitched in by a heavenly mother for first day of Koranic school.

Would it comfort you to know
That dust by dust she carved Milkman's ghost?
The book's discreet face & a twig in *Kumpo mask*.
Punctuate infinite drawings on the wall.
The Herdsman Mustapha & his gifts. Tender. But not tenderly.

If we could only look back at slavery, we would see ourselves,
Dying faithfully in Agadès. For hunger. The Sahara desert.

Kerosene lamp. My lustrous accent cracks. Multifold to death.
I chose summer in Casamance. June is burning high.
Je ne pardonnerai pas l'esclavage et l'holocauste.
Nous attendons civilisation sans peur.
Learning from bees. I meet vultures. To venture a holy spring.

If we could only look back at race,
We will see how it destroyed a nation's childhood.

When wandering owls reveal themselves
Like big black spikes. Restrained to the base of my tongue.
In a *Picasso Noir*, I begged for my Senegalese face to be left alone.
I failed (some kind of unfriendly meeting) with Jesus.

In the boundless sweat and sadness of winter
Monsters roar: grow your black hair for a blanket.
I starved myself to make room for Ghost Mother.

Dear Zainab Nafissatou,

Coffin Maker went to the Shrine to surrender. He has surrender. Coffin Maker has surrender. Villagers know. Villagers demolished the tunnel. Villagers have my tunnel of freedom. I hid your letters there. We are ready to hunker in the cassava garden where the devil can't find our bodies in blackness. They have learned that I hid Yara in the tunnel. Uncle Omar Mouhamed Cheikh's worries. A village is dying. Black bodies are trapped in a wasteland for sale. Hungry and weak bodies feed themselves soggy mud. Art of survival. Bodies use soggy mud & mask themselves, too. *Mon âme est comme un crépuscule Sénégalais.* Chaos surroundings a mango-vendor. The village's butcher meets a black woman. They listen to the river. For the dead and their lovers. Ghost Mother's beauty is black. She begs children to stay, for it is a painful business to see them leave. Orphan boys no longer preach, nor even beg. Welcoming children into a revolution. A wish for joy. Silence. For my uncle. *Degnmey Jonkal Bignona ak yalla khamna dama ragual kankouranrou Casamance ak deumeuyii nék Dakar.* Boys beg, for rice and blankets. Doing everything without a mother's protection. Demanding daggers. Daggers and hatchets. These days they sharpen such weapons on elephant tails collected long ago. They are soldiers festooned with shells and stones. Not blessed with Koranic verse. Diamond crucifixes hang from their necks. On sunny days, displaced mothers and daughters gather blankets and empty buckets. Leaving their dolls behind. Boats are waiting. These workwomen bend their fingers to pray. *Maison d'Arrêt de Reubeus: chambre 12.* Telling fathers who did not cross borders. Keep trying. Keep trying. Pain spoiling their torn headscarves. They sponge away their tears. Wait for Coffin Maker to measure our black bodies. *La grâce Sénégalaise.* They sing. They pray. It is hot even under the baobab. Before we meet for *Beugeureub.* A nude body suffers. A nude father and his girl drowned at the border. They did not hear the river. Ghost Mother's face is icy. She hates seeing Coffin Maker doing measurements of their bodies. Ways Coffin Maker cuts wood for black bodies. I comfort *her* & give *her* words of joy,

about the stranger's kiss

about burned black bodies

set carefully in pits

in boats

in banks

in prisons

                              in deprived schools
                              delivering all matter of life
                    among the village plants & wood
ghosts trapped on the trunk of a mango tree
                      in the sacred square of the cassava garden
                              terror
                              plunges
against exiled silence   I am silence   I am silence
bodies restrained unfaithfully
        drawing our secrets in exiled mud   I was mud
Calebasses. Orage. Kenosha. La mort. Poussière. Les bêtes. Nous. Les nègres mortels.
Nous. Les nègres d'Allah.
Nous. Les vrais sang de l'Amérique. Nous. Les vrais sang de la France.
                                                      I am still mud

                  from our long dark bodies
                              grief   America   black death.

Dandelion in Verandah

I

As if dandelion can't bloom where baobabs grow!
Dent-de-lion speaks, *alors, je m'invite á ôter mes*
Carcasses dans un charnier raciste.   It is a contest that
Rinsed Africa. *Fagarù balla gnùy tasù.* Its veil of bareness. Mud & memories.

This battle, a song, *a tribal* song, Doudou N'Diaye Rose *ak Sabar.*
A passage of unknown with the doorways of no return.
Deum yii nawaal sama fiit neema loo ragual da lay gaagnë.

To understand our progress, through isolated spaces;
Years to complete a history. It is not stress-free. *Mbalax.*
You do not open your heart. What remains in Ghost Mother's faith.

In our childhood voices. Our grief is also our anxiety. It belongs to our bodies.
We have it masked between our white teeth & the bones of our jaws.
Hamdoulilah, gnowleen fëgg, gnowleen sëgg gnowleen mëgg deum yii.

II

The village's *Tëgg* said, it is not a sickness. What is it the dandelion conveys to Us?
Our wisdom is in between the baobabs' roots of freedom time,
"Nobody paid Us any attention, so we paid very good attention to ourselves."
For the burial of the wooden Jar. Coffin Maker did not attend!

No, your scramble for Africa. Can't trace our history, *nos murs sont pendus*!
Dirt, not freedom. *De la mort et ni du vent exilé des fantômes*!

Ghost Mother carries black-tongued stars. So orphaned. They stand
All night to witness in a wide stance. I re-wound scars in the webs of my back
To keep my ancestors in their ghosts company in burned cotton fields.
Alors. Très bien. Dieu te punit. Esprit colonialiste. Quitte l'Afrique. Quitte l'Afrique.

III

Weeping. Vines crumble in green. The verandah had moist mud.
For my African skin. But I wait to scale dry blood, raw as a black death.
I use it to smear yolk stains. As a form of betrayal.
Let it blossom. Imam said, before he blessed Us,
It is asked once: whose freedom are we celebrating?

Dear Houriyya,

Wounds on Ghost Mother's back have healed, *Alhamdulillah*! Villagers want you to leave your native village. A ruler wants you to leave your native village. Black scars on Ghost Mother's belly. Flashed in a broken mirror. Savage me keep silent with *Kumpo*. It helped me compose a new habit. So, I may tend the cows carrying black babies and *Sabar*. *Tëgg* and Senegalese history in the tunnel of *Îls de Gorée*. Your lonely body falls alone *ak Sabar*. Your lonely body is lynched alone. A polished African mask from Senegal. *Fagarù balla gnùy tasù*. Here pride meets winter's grief. It is a village where it once rained nails. A blind girl was burned in a shed. Her mother was out pleading in front of the mosque. *"Imam, little thoughts can harm big thoughts,"* said the mother. She went and sat in front of the mosque. Chewing on a toothpick. Until she suddenly stood up and opened the mosque doors wide. *Degnmey Jébbal Tabaski gnoume gneupeu gneuw gnou feck-fa harbi mou wowe conk*. Today is June 26, 1991. It marks a second anniversary of a black body killed in the middle of a forgotten city. In destroyed cities, roots of secret flowers live forever. *Maison d'Arrêt de Reubeus: chambre 25*. Mother, your dear friend Houriyya, was released yesterday from her 20 years of hunger strike. She is released by the ruler. I am recalling what you said about Fatoumata. How she is a spirit of our village. I remember she came out when colonizers took over church & mosque. You sat at your kitchen table listening to her wish. Listening to her hope. Listening to her fury. You both had agreed that politics was mud. That politics was meanness. That politics was burns on blind girl's chest. Was Houriyya's husband Coffin Maker? Was Houriyya's husband Imam? Was Houriyya's husband the village's *Tëgg*? In a village now, we learned that Coffin Maker had told Imam about his wife. She and *Sabar* climbed up into a mango tree to keep owls company. She saw Imam heading for the brook, carrying a rope and a white chair. No evening prayers. A girl named Mariama decomposed herself for peace during wartime

         asking rebels to forgive and forget
      return to bless a village &
   to meet
         Coffin Maker's wife: a terrible old story
         nations'
treasures of black bodies *Dieu te punit*: so we trap the devil and the thieves
               Lubnâ says: no sunset prayers
      villagers will burn themselves   &   go to court

                    we proceed inside a
          dusty chamber,
                    where seized girls
             share
                              chosen feelings
          with tender scorpions
not in America (of course…)   *Alhamdulillah,*
                    you knew your body's tribe
Alhamdulillah   you knew   you   were   landing   with
    vulnerability   &   your naked body
                                        Sarah Baartman

    for a dictator's unholy orgasm.

Milkman's Widow

I lit a kerosene lamp.
Bilay wallah I could not see by it.   Years ago. Multiple ways of seeing the self.
The hunger for pictures of my childhood   a strange childhood.
Mango-picking   given heavy rain   Milkman was there.   I was poor.
For a full week.   Still broken from Ghost Mother's death. Unable to
Arrange a past life & carrying the burden of defeat   exile.
I have an African fragrance and I embrace its opaque aroma.
It is impossible to live an ordinary life.   I am forever alienated.
This is a place   a home & a cassava garden.   outsider in America.
I stepped in   step by step.   To please her.   torn shoes.   They
Are mine.   Removed before her veranda *entrée*.
Through old holy books. Photos & bundle of diaries.   Gathered carefully.
Ghost Momma says, "I might not have been born in the United States. I might
  not have inherited the trauma and the tragedy that black Americans have who
                    come from enslaved ancestry."
Too late to question my own devotion.   Reports of genocide in Senegal.
Savage me keep silent.   She helped me compose a new habit.
So,   I may tend the cows carrying black babies   &   history in the
tunnel of harmony in Osu Castle, Timbuktu & Gorée.
Cows crossing borders.   Looking at a slave death in complete faith.
In our bodies   Ghost Mother of wisdom knows how to sense the devil's secret.

We agreed. Milkman's graft is difficult.
Who knew what Milkman did?   With the devil.
If he saw everything.   He did not see the dead's return.
                    In pitch dark. Who realized Milkman knew the
devil's   language?
                    A kerosene lamp in his home had become
Too bright for Milkman's widow:
                she suffered from grief & her lonely black body. Upon
                arrival,
passports are confiscated. I forget a first return to my roots.   Milkman
wounded by his own cows.
          Milkman's widow could not speak, except tenderly.
                              voices played dead from her oozing. Her
          chamber is on fire. That was all.

Dear Yandé Codou Sène,

You said colonizing the mind was not human. My God! Your tolerance for the village's Shrike Keeper. Massamba failed the village. *Hamdoulilah*, you said hanging Massamba, the Keeper of the Shrine was a sin. Elders came to your home to warn you. My God! *Fatou Diome, diambaroo Senegal ack Tamam ack xéleum bou saf sap nii kouroussou serigne Touba*. You called the vultures and the owls. With your crying. Vultures and owls came. Packing up black bodies. Hung black bodies from a lonely railway bridge. Hung black bodies in lonely plantations. It was May 25, 1911. You are haunted by slung bodies. A slung black mother & her black boy. With your crying, I feel touched. I can be touched. I am touched. For years I have been lost learning a new tongue. Modern me worries. I want to be westernized. Before my body is traumatized. Wounded. I taught myself this new tongue called English. I want to teach a body how to camouflage itself from traps. The way we camouflage the self in language. A body knows death is safe. A body learning how to move beyond pinned borders. You said, I have given everything for my new tongue. Ghost Mother, I hope to caress your heart with this new tongue. It is the only weapon I have. It is the only wisdom I have. The civilized tribes. Welcome *us* & *Sūrat: Al-Nas* & *Al-Fatihah*. In my eyes, I am providing one kind of bounded vision. A self-conscious wisdom. The Milkman's devices for you. He forgot to bring Jesus's Cross. Your devices for calling on the vultures. To clean up rotten flesh. To tell vultures to clean up dust, dusk & mud. You told vultures to clean up nature. *Bilay wallah*, you told vultures to clean up earth. Of course, I can't explain. We are crowded with strangers. On boulevards a fuss over old stones. *Je me suis mise à aimer un village dangereux. La nature même de ce que j'écris*. But village bricklayers are on strike. You are seeing father at church. Father is healed by Jesus and the thieves. Father heals by your crying and the vultures. It's been years since I smelled mud. *Je suis le fils du défunt*. They once mixed it for my destroyed childhood. My useful hunger woke Ghost Mother from her sleep…

today is Friday, August 9, 2014, *America.*
Dieu te punit. Dieu te punit. Dieu te punit. Dieu te punit.

after prayers   for a black death
Coffin Maker measures

empty yards behind a
girls' school to   build another grave
for Ghost Mother   and   a black death—
mother's sister
(my aunt)—   is our village
a spirit now, she asks me to carve the

                              names of saints & Senegalese smiles
                    I don't know on its gates
            the village   wants to call our school
                    something   I don't know   writing I can't read
they say   they say   they say, do not worry   they say, they say to call the village's
Tëgg

                                        we are on the lookout
                        we won't let sick
                girls   dig through
                    compost & dumpsters behind
        the   hospital
they say   they won't let sick girls   cross borders.

Decolonized Machine

The foundation of
my deportation
came when
Ghost Mother
    took
    her
    own.

Ghost Mother said, "*Nĕkkinam bä foufä neexul kenn ci gnŭn!*"
Des claques sur ta bouche. Esprit colonialiste. Alors. Très bien. Je te défit !

The home, she bought in classified bazaars,
they say the color of Ghost Mother's skin is sour
401 years later, she is not allowed even today,

in locked away neighborhoods, where
ghosts of gentrification are baptized in mud & in devil's water.

Mon abaissement ! *Je te défit* ! *Quitte l'Afrique*! *Dieu te punit.*

Gated fields,
festooned with fence posts
on which the 1st, 2nd, 13th & 14th amendments
dangled grotesquely to zero,
but fear of my sable skin.

Ses larmes sur ma face ténébreuse.

From Senegal, New York City to Missouri,
dark clouds come hurrying with an aloof wind
turning abruptly: me & officer X baptizing violence.
I can't speak. My body in his Americanized machine.

Le silence ! *Fermes ton bec. Mes claques sur ta bouche. Esprit colonialiste.*
Monde de malheur. Esprit colonialiste. Je te défit. Quitte l'Afrique.

Officer X's madness chasing alarms for blackness,
before I am told to leave the zone.

It is said, "I opened my mouth to say,
I don't what. When I opened my mouth,
I couldn't catch my breath" to breathe in Americanized devices.

Dear Issa Ndèye Coumba,

You said, Jesus came with language for desire & faith. We came with vultures & sacred mud. Milked our black skin-skinned selves. Before curfew. The streets are shut & we are heading to the mosque. You said what about Ghost Mother & Uncle Omar Mouhamed Cheikh? Were you one of the midwives? Who forgot to clean the blood? Babies died, you blessed them. For you, vultures came for days & nights waiting at the church's entrance. For no one called them. There was not enough blood. But vultures came. Here I am telling: I don't know who. Are you blue? Are you black? Momma gone for that big & beautiful Senegalese smile. Even when they are fasting, midwives work. Their care seemed to last even longer than time itself. Did you bless village newborns? You encouraged new mothers not to worry. *Ajuuma la tey nit demna wax nit dox bi dof bi wax bi dox na wax na sabar nee dëgg tee xelal niit.* There are tolerant owls longing for a quiet wind on mango trees. There are no tolerant vultures. We don't know how to call them. Or attend to them. Coffin Maker used to watch girls bring water in buckets from distant well. Nurses scrubbing new mother's blood. You are what our village has hoped for. You whispered *surahs: Al-Mu'minoon* & *Al-Qalam* in newborn ears. You are prompt as death. I don't know about owls and mango trees. You said, "go home or go to your mosque." You said, "go home or go to your church." You are keepers of menstrual secrets. Ghost Mother said the priest is not helping. You must know that Ghost Mother cures newborns of every disease. I dream in *Wolof* and write in English. I am a lone companion hugging black sorrow. Slave master says no matter what I do I won't be free. Slave master has signed me up. *Yay boy* knows newborns' discomfort & discomfort of their mothers. *Je me suis mise à aimer mon village au pays natal.* Grief is in a village cemetery where village donkeys under a perky sun are trotting in my ribcage. I can't even read Milkman's dairies filled with his sacred devices. Skin & my muddy tongue, I am less, master says. In mud, I weep again. Milkman's sacred dairy. I weep again. I weep again. Black ribcages have been aching for years. Last evening, before I removed shackles. Shackles injure my dead body. Shackles took away a pride I'll never recover. I wrote a note for a slave master,

    between muddy huts & fences, I am dying to   say-so   being free
  on duty for the killing   it left   me   to consider
        how to live   living is wanting to be
                        on my prayer rug
                  a crucifix does work

masking itself   violating   your sketches & sceneries   literature
    using   excessive   force   to   search   for   answers
                        I have to wait to rinse my feet
dung has caked up in between   my toes   &   my passport died in exile
I worry   how to escape   the cruelty   of my   master
here   armed to kill   my God!   fatal encounters
                                with flowers and black candles to
                    place on mother's grave
    I am lost   &   messy   &   bleeding everywhere
                                I have been restrained for years
                    my black body is numb &
                God knows what
                    when master catches   a fled body
                    dying slowly
                        two nuns chant my name
    once   Ghost Mother asked me to tip my African masks: *Kumpo* &
Kankourang,

                        solemnly
                I fear but live on with *Sabar, Tama* & *Xalam.*

Dear Momma,

Vultures came to witness *Beugeureub*. My body. A polished disaster. We danced with Jesus. Slaves. Our tribe. The sacred songs. The exiled. My body is where pride meets winter's grief. My body is in a village where it once rained mud. My body is where a little blind boy was trapped. My body was in a burning shed while you were out begging for dirt. Begging for milk & a soccer ball. Begging for papers. Begging for mud from the Nile. Begging for candles & *Challah* bread. Begging for a lawyer in Memphis, Tennessee.

My body witness a public disagreement no one had ever seen. It is said, "nothing is sacred any longer and nothing is appropriate for a body anymore." My body told the Imam. My body and the dead body washer are not from the same faith. Momma bring me *Ceebu jënn ack Thiakry*. Momma can call for the prayer. I am begging for a judge, but Momma says, "I am alive and in my body." Momma says, "I am black alive and looking back at" Officer X in mud, then vultures came running.

My tongue is licking a prophet's sweat to heal the chameleon. My body was sharpened on the Koran's surface. Momma can call for the prayer. Mustapha, the Herdsman is not coming for tonight's *Nafilas* at the mosque.

My body climbed up into the baobab tree to keep owls, vultures, and snakes company. Momma saw the Imam heading for the Casamance River, carrying a rope and a small chair. Momma call for the prayer before Jesus! Jesus came for mud. Jesus came for Ghost Momma & Mustapha.

Abattoir Near Rice Farms

In the house in Senegal that morning,
A telephone rang.
It was Uncle Omar Mouhamed Cheikh calling.
Two floors above,
In the verandah,

Mother's ghost was
Unaware of the kerosene lamp,
& photos of my white Jewish mother:
Within saintly stars.
Ghost Mother says, it was August 9, 1997.

Where lizard & chameleon lick my blood,
spiders are equipped with authority,
J'ai brodé mes cauchemars
Dans les bords de l'Océan Atlantique.
Years later, I still hear that note
On my new tongue.

It was more like a savannah the
Villagers in my native village never forget.
Milkman was chewing Jesus's Wood
Or something that dissolved in *Bissap ack Bouye.*

I am outside. Rain is mud here. The village's *Tëgg* died!
At dusk, I light a campfire. And wait for vultures.
I lie on my back to watch the dead and their lovers.
It is said they count on the color of my skin & whiteness?
Ghost Mother's feminine touch and her neatness.
Ghost Mother's tidy ways mend my mood & my sickness.

Dear Laylâ,

Greetings, and here is a wish. You said my uncle no longer wants to live. His grief has torn him up. Grief for blind twins remain. *Dem démeuti góor wala baadolo jaamou Wolof bou saf sap jaam booy toye bounte keureum jaamou Diola boo xamadi, jaamou Peul, jaamou Socé, jaamou Lawbé Worworbé, jaamou Serer, baadolo dou lekkadi lekk lekatt.* Ghost Mother knew how to recover. Us, too, our bodies knew how to recover. Dead are way easier with their guardians. The dead and their nationalized dolls. Carrying ropes. Black plastic bags for chunks of black flesh. Plastic bags filled with flesh. Blind twins are ready for war. You warned Us to be aware of the vultures' neatness. Neatness of slaves' ships. They go to war with complete elegance. They are faithful, like the dead. Being faithful like a black death. Elders beg me to stop with Ghost Mother and stay away from the mosque & the church. I am not allowed in graveyards. Strangers hardly welcome a mother's tenderness. Its meaning. It is said, outsiders longing for freedom are not welcome. Jesus catechizes, the goals Ghost Mother sets for the Pope, the Nurses, France & America. Thieves are no longer welcome in our village *Alhamdulillah*! In our village, homes are festooned with flowers and the names of the dead. Jesus promises that a body is to be free. On Friday, I stand beside you. What you have been longing for. The evening prayers offer tenderness to me. You repeat God's prayers. Sob loudly with fax tears. Under the sun of the Dead Sea. You lead Us to the orphanage. I am concerned about the thieves and their health. Wounds. They conceal to get by. I am expelled from graveyards. I forgot books and Jesus's Water. I went back to look for books. Holy books. Ah! I forgot Coffin Maker locked them away forever. In the dimness of sunset. Land falls and leaves me near a slaughterhouse. I crossed borders to be free. My spirit thinks of Ghost Mother, and her lonely scars on her belly. Hunger ripens. As village peasants enter church. It is shut by neat thieves. They took black chairs swollen with grief. Uncle Omar Mouhamed Cheikh was sick again & Ghost Mother boiled roots,

Uncle Omar Mouhamed Cheikh's prayer beads   *beats*   violence
           I have never seen

a kerosene lamp dying a black death

       a bridge of sadness is pinned
         in my throat
       for years now killed because
it collapses   racing with clocks of the mosque
       its relation to the soil is simple

noble   &   direct
Ghost Mother is
company
for my lonely & poor body   quiet safe
service bodies once provided
bodies collapse for struggle *America. Dieu te punit.*
Dieu te punit. Dieu te punit. Dieu te punit.
I am outside Friday prayer   boundless
waiting for arrival of *Kumpo* & *Kankourang*
waiting for dispatch
I count on blackness   Village's *Tëgg*   Coffin Maker
&   Uncle Omar Mouhamed Cheikh
Ghost Momma strikes a pose to stand over a landscape before she cupped a
land of the free in her holy hands, before she   votes
arriving   from   no where   America.

Ghost Mother's Note

A black woman's image was master's only instructor.
J'ai mes mains rouges de sang!
Here is a ticket to see the volatile works of Coffin Maker.
I am sickened by his swelling forehead.
The smell of wood in his workshop. Blood at its doorknob.

He controlled the textbook
Of my lost childhood. *Hamdoulilah.*
It is said Coffin Maker slept face down
On a rooming verandah floor. Humming to moist mud.
One mode he used to discipline his illness.

He dreamt against the cold & the Shrine Keeper never came.
Hills & owls, masked in plants from a holy desert,
To clean up my childhood. Vultures remain.
I lean my left hand to promise sadness & expired medicines,

Before the trailing whiteness,
Says, *go back to Africa, you native monkey.*
There is no other way back to Senegal.
Gorée Island is where freed slaves
Go to claim what's left of Africa.
Tam tam: is French, drums.

Sounds of *Tam tam* are barking to curse
Jefferson's cargo of slaves. *Hamdoulilah.*
Of papers signed for darkness to travel
Restrained, at high sea. From Cuba, Jamaica, Colombia to Brazil.

Dear God, I wonder. How to wonder.
Tried to imagine what it must have felt like
To find myself chained up & wordless.
Wordless in its melancholic sense.
Not being able to speak my *Wolof, Bambara & Diola*?

On my way to where? Haiti, Martinique, America?
Ghost Mother left me with a hole I can't fill.
Her death have me grieving for years.
Her death is a revenge that is unlawful.

Dear Christiane Mame-Ngoné,

Greetings. It was a cold evening. February 4, 1999. You said, my broken childhood keeps me going. You said, I was baptized with water the devil can't touch. In the village rice farms. Sugarcane farms. Rice farms burn for a bitter dose. Black bones & mud from African shores. What they release. Where I come from. Ghost Mother was not in the sewage this evening. Owls' bones liberate the body. What they carried. What the Officer X asked them. What border patrols ask me. Lonely days of youth ruined. But what it lit. Bodies, what they suffered. Bodies, what they touched! *Dama gàddu adunaa sama bopp ak sama ndogalou yala. Americain wala toubab loo xam cëe kumpo wala kankourang.* But first, portrait as Ghost Mother. It's eleven years since I last smelled it. Pearls in her headscarf give villains sunlight they can't read in the dark. At evening, she praises stubbornness of baobab. She leaves Dakar for heaven. She takes red candles and blankets. To the mosque & all tenderness blooms in sugarcane farms. I would starve myself to see her in dreams. When a black boy screams "I Have a Dream." Morning grace in my lonely body asks me. It is said, are you American. I said. How can I not be American? What does it have to do with being an American? Being American is difficult. I know my history & it speaks to Americanness. Mother knows obscure owls and their secrets. *Je vois Sénégal qui change la couleur de mon désir.* Baobab tree from Senegal (did you know inside it / bees make honey, oil for village children?) Black mamba rest through its branches. Keeping the evil serpent away. Chicken danced cheerfully underneath the baobab's peaceful shade. Elders debated about harvest & bridal. Evil brought the dead. Elders are unable to evade the bad spirits in the village. So, they call the Ghost Mothers. Elders mourn for you. Elders morn for bodies. You grieved for black dead bodies. You asked elders. Who needs to donate to the mosque & the church? Upcoming rainy season. All I remember was being circumcised. Resting there with rain. A body so innocent. It is blackened by secrets buried underneath America's speech. What does it have to do with our case? A body hid itself behind a Senegalese mask. A place. A border. A refugee. Will you have whiteness mourn for a body? Ghost Mother said I don't belong here,

learning a prisoner's rule   where a guard beats me
        to disguise a body   to disguise my wounds, I call on
Ghost Mother to weep   every   night for help
                                she is sick, crying at night
                        she is dying
    I cut myself   to bleed a little
                letting black blood out
                                            to keep her alive
                        we have been waiting for a doctor
a doctor never came instead
                                    instead   I offer   mother
                fresh baobab leaves   to chew
        so to cure her   from satisfying   her needs
                                        baobab's shells
I use to make   vessels for Ghost Mother's sacrament
                                here I built music of my tribe
                accepting Koran to heal Us
            singing *Al- Israa'*
so we let it turn in slaves' hymns & Jesus's Lyrics
    I die before America's divine history when mud was bloody & the ghosts
    your violence burning up the block.

Dear Momma,

Bilay wallah, my body knows what nothing does to death. It knows what death does to memories. My body is in a violent gust of wind that shatters all the sacred tribes. My body is left in a wrecked Senegalese / American boy. My body is a blind boy walking along Broadway. *Momma* hears my humble prayer. My body knows that usually monsters are the outsiders here. My body knows they are from a different race. They are from a different tribe. My body is *Diola* and *Wolof.* My body knows the malevolent being. *Gnac ka laaj sama xamxam. Je te défit. Je te défit. Je te défit. Je te défit. Je te défit. Je te défit. Esprit colonialiste. Quitte l'Afrique.*

My body walks toward the sea for faith. My body loses its memories with each step. Nonetheless, my body hopes to wash away its bitterness. My body arrives through shipwreck, at the gates of the sea. The harpy mother hands my body an envelope of disease to deliver to a father. *Je suis le fils du défunt. Je suis le fils du défunt. Je suis le fils du défunt. Je suis le fils du défunt. Quitte l'Afrique. Quitte l'Afrique.*

Even with the Koran wide-open beside his bed, my body knows a father's wound grows and becomes a tumor. In a father's giant wound, spiders sharpen their legs. *Bilay wallah*, my body strikes at freedom. *Bilay wallah*, my body is wounded in America. Kneeling before Jesus's Cross. And Slaves' songs. Ghost Momma said, she has "lived as a black person in" America. Ghost Momma said, she has "lived as a mother raising black children" in America.

Dear Khartoum,

We whispered to the girls in *Wolof* to say, *that there was no food.* We told them. The Pope came with Jesus. They said, the dead black bodies in the streets of America have been blessed.

Coffin Maker's blown-off toolbox is gone. His historic toolbox has been stolen. Coffin maker's devices for pleasing the dead is gone. We told them, the soup Aunt Khartoum made at dawn before Coffin Maker's ballad has gone bad. Coffin Maker sprung up in a Casamance wilderness. Deadly rice farms. The deadly jungles in Casamance. Coffin Maker has been a slave, I was told. Ghost Mother wept on the first day of Ramadan to set him free. Coffin Maker's wounds on his back. Arrived from: *Tam Tam* who greets *Sabar, Xalam* and *Tama,* in *Wolof.* Uncle Omar Mouhamed Cheikh said, *Jaam nga fanan khamo lou saa mameboy guiss.* You said, America allowed, our two hostile bodies and the third one to surrender. The outcasts are misread. Us. We surrender for history. Ghost Mother said, America let Us out naked, cool & black. For history. America let Us lick a white master's flogging device. You said, for history. The cold "Founding Fathers spilled blood that will never dry" in the streets of America & France. To let blood camouflage our stained pride. *Pourtant, Il a de la tendresse, et le Wolof, pour prononcer. Les Diables de l'Amérique. Les Diables de la France.* So cold now, a body is black. So hostile now, a skin is pale. So frail now, a baobab's trunk is square. Coffin Maker's blood is composed of gallant ghosts. My God. His gifts. Knowing how to please the dead. Knowing how to please the dead and their folks. Knowing what kind of wood would please the dead. Knowing how to split the spine of wood. Knowing what time of the day is best for cutting wood. Devoting days & hours tending a coffin. When he skinned and wrenched off rottenness from his work. Moistness and worms from his work are pealed with Ghost Mother's elegance. One of the Ghost Mothers—Nima Elbagir's courage—her blessings. Her neatness is a gift for Us. The exiled black bodies. Coffin Maker graced a coffin's spine to please the dead. Ghost Mother said, Coffin Maker is from the *Diola* tribe. This story I won't tell you. But Coffin Maker always knew when, the dead of the summer arrive to flatten the meadow. In my dreams, baobab roots are boiled for Ghost Mother to heal her placenta. She has been sick for years. To cure my loose & deadly American accent before sunrise. American-ness is exiled until full moon! It has

been since I returned to her grave. On my arrival. It was August heat. I watched
Auntie Khartoum from a sunlit hole-in-the-wall. Ghost Momma & the Pope
held hands to bless the exiled black bodies. Us & our crooked narrative history.
Whiteness don't recall in detail. It is alright. America we came to say forever.
Listen. Listen. It is alright just listen. We have Ghost Momma. Maybe I was
a bush boy with no Food Stamp. On the muddy verandah, so poor & licking
moist mud. At sunset, Coffin Maker waited with broken coffins. I am not tell-
ing you why or how.   Bush boy said…   his masked   frame   died
off   into the blue   of his
     tender   black skin   the Pope, Ghost Momma & Coffin Maker said,
               we may want to meet the *mukhtâr* in *Bayda* to ask for peace,
                         & praise the black bodies
nightmares   drunken   baby bats   owls   snakes   porcupines   &
     reindeer / vultures   *Tëgg's* red iron   Coffin Maker & his moist wood
wedding   our cry   to explore hostile rivers
his disgraced   memories… it is said…   guards patrolling   the borders
     have been up all night   drunk from mud   &
     sweat from our black bodies, hugging   *Sick Goat's* horn,   for blessings
                         gently   it is said…   dear America
                    we outgrow everything   aren't we too history?
when our spines snap   threatening
     alabaster
oblique   freely   at sea.

82

Multinational Self

Imagine shutting myself in the American face,
where I face the low slung & pale sky to draw
everywhere African-ness begun Negro-ness to end
the elephant's shadow of *Négritude*.
Poivrons doux et piments dans mes blessures.

The will to smile that big Senegalese smile-
Un Homme blanc me dépose au regard de
L'Océan Atlantique, au regard des terres Africaines!
Because I refuse to stop for prose.

Because the aches of double exile never froze.
My humming lure vultures in jungles for a saintly dose.
We slowly become French, Senegalese/American in the law of faith.
The setting of dreams gone dark on bamboo farms.

Les secrets de la Mère Fantôme.
Du Tchouraï pour déloger le mal.
Du Tchouraï pour purifier sa véranda boueuse.

Looking back, insanity and nostalgia curve against
my people's tongues (*tu penses dangereux*) in defense
of multinational self a penance I pay for Coffin Maker.
Je suis le mendiant béni. Je suis le mendiant guéri.

It is said, I was baptized in the Shrine with *Kumpo*. Church was shut.
Through the rebels' attack, Ghost Mother knew it was safe.
Gän bou doxot balay leck deem rootii deerett ack dem dëe.
Au cœur des vautours. Sable. Boue. Rivières. Fleurs. Plantes.
Mais. Alors. Très bien. Je te défit. Esprit colonialiste. Je te défit. Quitte l'Afrique !

Dear Mame Fatou Kiné,

Once a Senegalese trilogy was outlawed, you said. Milkman said, he knew the tragedy that happened to Mustapha. The Herdsman. Because Milkman was no longer a sacred person in my village. He was no longer a sacred relic. His farms and shrines have been ruined. Burned to black. He called, but I told him it was too late. America is my (new home). Milkman *dima enquête si téléphonebi sama yérem dow*! *Té-khamouma kagn lay gnibissi kagn lay gnibi Sénégalo*! You said, the court for expats does not care for West African returnees. Uncle Omar Mouhamed Cheikh said, *Tam-Tam- (sabar) music Sénégalaise des années imaginaires.* He said, from our dark faces, grow fear & one broken mask in many broken masks. By *deportee*, my uncle said, French and before Senegal 1960, what did the French take with them to France? Whether I recalled how Milkman conquered my dream. In the emperor's strange illness. Silent & melancholic at the sea. I sink with an old rebel chief. His *Wolof* and *Diola* tongues are difficult. He flowers in oblique dialect. Wasn't loneliness the knowledge to cure exile. Double exile strikes and kills every union of expats. Dying a shameful death. He asked, Milkman said, yes. To pardon a corrosive guilt. Milkman said, he civilized. What I learned in the Koranic school. Anxieties. When I trace the moon's spine with my wooden slate in *Wolof.* To see how Ghost Mother clouds in the vessel of my new home. That was when I knew. I am, I am, I am not destroyed. Looking like what? Milkman said, I was broken in mud. You said, I am baptized by the household snake, *Kankourang,* Jesus and *Kumpo mask.* You said, I am uprooted by devices that nursed my raw exile. You said. *Cette nuit de nostalgie accablée. Nostalgie amputée. Crime de ses nostalgies.* Identical to my faithful grief. Echo by echo. Voice by voice. Verb by verb. Noun by noun. *l' Amérique avale mon sang noir et me brûle tout nu.* Milkman's portrait in Casamance in 1994… drowned in deluge. *Bilay wallah …* Ghost Mother said. That was the year

    the year she heard

        an aged man cry for real in Missouri & Nairobi   *Bilay wallah*, it was
                Milkman on a Friday
           it was when the rebels did not attack villagers
                Ghost Mother had just finished
                          rearranging
           Uncle Omar Mouhamed Cheikh's basement
                which Fatou Kiné
        my aunt   hoarded
                with her American goods

                receipts   notices   doctor's notes   forms
Je te défit. Je te défit. Je te défit. Je te défit. Je te défit. Je te défit. Esprit colonialiste. Quitte
l'Afrique!
The Rabbi & Ghost Momma said...
American innocence. Evil deeds. Dust. Jefferson. Sally Hemings. The six children.
Founding Fathers. Lies. The American way.
                vouchers
                        American drugs   expired   American drugs
                                        papers papers papers
                                Uncle Omar kept things, too
letters   papers and of course   his   filthy and sacred working
        clothes   American papers
                holy   ashes   they   are   souvenirs
                                to be handled   in my new home
                to be handled in a home of one's own   a slave owner.

85

IN SHRINE

When I die in the streets of America,
My traumatized skin must be endorsed like Master's allegiance.
For whipping me. Knock knock who's there. Milkman.
Milkman is not more African than I (spare you from death!)
Of the Senegalese slave howling, a haunting sob is better
Than a bamboo flute's—crying to ghosts—from the Nile.
One kind of myth. Fistfuls of mud. *Kankourang's* mask.
Ah! my father's broken promise & his wish for ruined results!
In my immaculate *kaftan*, Ghost Mother gives me fresh milk.
It was August. Circumcised beside the river. Burning heat.
I treasure. Ô! I declare. Possibly being "the outsider" is safer.
J'ai l'impression d'être déracinée. Le faucou. Drunk from palm oil.
I would want to see dry blood in my gaping wounds burst & burn.
Cuts caused by a stung master in the meadow. *La crise des langues.*
Le vautour dévorant son ombre. L'aigle royal. Drunk from *Bissap.*
Bush boy's shrine contained sacred relics when it broke.

Dear Momma,

It is said you nurture dusk and the holy desert *Alhamdulillah*! It is said you blessed me with vultures and hyenas, *Alhamdulillah*! It is said that you nurture cassava garden and mud *Alhamdulillah*! You said. We do not deceive. Dying even restrained at high sea. Momma you said, dying like a ghost. It was restrained for the blessed crowd to witness. The raven and the vulture. The camel and the donkey. Fairness & harmony in our village. At the mosque & in church. It is said you nurture hyenas' bones *Alhamdulillah*! It is said you nurture Senegalese owls and their journeys at night. Don't tell *them* Founding Fathers. Details of black feathers in a middle of jungles. Milkman said, vultures and his clients don't go to prison. Milkman said, his son Yara will not beat his case. Because vultures came for blood and red meat. Everyone desire's absence. Uncle Omar Mouhamed Cheikh said *Alhamdulillah*! You are linking to the universal. Can you imagine Officer X protecting *Kompo* & *Kankourang*. *Bilay wallah*, can you imagine Office X protecting Yara? Ghost Mother said, judge my boy he did not do it! Even if a price on our heads. It is said, it was important for Yara's case. When he asked, where was his judge. Each body still throbbing broken to black & dying tolerantly. Coffin Maker said, *In-challah*! Hyenas, vultures, owls, and his clients will never do a double homicide. The unknown for the end of hunger. Shrine Keeper said, don't tell *them* Founding Fathers. How we nurture vultures. How we care for mud and hunger. You said, even if restrained alive and dying a black death. You said, we are not born in the USA. You said, we come to the USA. You said, we become the USA. You said, we are the USA. You said, judge my boy he did not do it! A scene. Vultures in mud. A dream. Nurses and their hunger. Restrained alive & dying a black death. Americanized for violence. Of course. We learned in the Atlantic. Vultures in the *abattoir* decomposing our dreams. History and milk. About a woman. A black woman's former lover. Dust in the holy desert. Blood hung in flowers only in destroyed cities. About a French woman. Ghost Momma said, is it Passover. We have wine and matza. Sacred ghosts in the synagogue. Drunk from honey. We wait for Coffin Maker & the Rabbi to bless Us. The Rabbi came with *Challah* bread. Ghost Momma gone. We lit candles to read our wounds. The Rabbi came during Rosh Hashanah to bless Us. From the dream. We hunger ourselves in the Marais. The Rabbi came to hunger with Us before we enter Place des Vosges. After prayer hour: hunger ripens in

America, but the Rabbi bless Us. His work is the holiest. He gave me ghosts and a hunter's gift. My God! The Rabbi's gifts. Watching over Us. He curse American violence. The evening he came to light the menorah with Us. Prayers, Rabbi gave to Us. Rabbi came bearing gifts: latke, sour cream & applesauce from the holy land. Rethinking Hanukkah through the Rabbi. Is a blessing! My limbs swung inside my dark skin. Ghost Momma stooped at the door to pray for my holy body to return home safely. Ghost Momma kneeled near Jesus to beg for my safe return. Ghost Momma was pleading to the judge. When her tears & her sweaty hands sealed a Jesus's Cross. Ghost Momma said, "American violence is learned violence. It is the American way." Jesus's Milk is dripped for my departure. My arrival will be a beginning. My arrival is a beginning. I came with blessings. Mud, black blood, gracious as a slave. You said, *Sūrat al Fātihah.* Never. Never. Never. *Tell them cold Founding Fathers where.* We buried nightmares and hyenas' bones in the cassava garden & how I live up the absurd. The Herdsman and his gifts. Everywhere, in my country of birth, you said, a hunter is black. I will not tell *them* this story. Late from my prayers. But you said, I have *Sūrat al Balad* and *Sūrat al Falaq.* I am amazed to discover. Officer X is in my nightmares. But in this awful nightmares. I reimagined. My Blackness. My slaveness. Decolonizing Officer X. Working in the farm. Housekeepers. Papers given. The Italian way. Oozing for the cold weather. Alcohol cloths. The devil in my hospital bed. The Pope came for a slave reason. I am amazed to discover that you have gone & Jesus came. But that from the cassava garden. From the exact spot of the burial. In the cassava garden. I could hear words you whispered. I could hear you praised the Lord. The prayers you asked Jesus. The prayers you asked *Allah*! The prayers you asked *Yéesus.*

Adieu.

II

Gratitude and Acknowledgments

Infinite gratitude is due to my family members in Senegal and New York City for their kindness, support, and love. For the countless times you sparked my imagination. For the dark times when you lifted my soul and gave me shelter. For the home and love you give. For the light, grace and comfort you brought in my dark times. Your power and kindness is forever honored.

Thank you to the following magazines in which some of the poems originally appeared:

Free Verse: A Journal of Contemporary Poetry & Poetics: special thanks to Jon Thompson.

The *Ampersand* at Washington University in St. Louis: special thanks to Claire Gauen.

Transverse: special thanks to the Centre for Comparative Literature at the University of Toronto.

Thanks are also due to these extraordinary folks: the one and only Lucie Brock-Broido, Susan Bernofsky, Richard Howard, J. Dillon Brown, Timothy Donnelly, Lynne Tatlock, Carolyn Durham, Daniel Bourne, Bruce Smith, Francine J. Harris, Shane McCrae, Vincent Sherry, Ignacio Infante, Dominique Combe, Ayo A. Coly, Mary Jo Bang, Claudia Rankine (for reading *Owls of Senegal*), Derek Gromadzki, Eleni Philippou, Matthew Reynolds, Matthias Goeritz, Roger Reeves, Odile Poncy, Marc Jeanson, Bruce Smith, Dominique Darbon, Sylvere Mbondobari, Alan Gilbert, Carl Phillips, Andrés Claro, Pablo Oyarzún Robles, Jane O. Newman, Cole Swensen, and my *hero* Ngugi wa Thiong'o.

To my colleagues in the International Writers program at Washington University in St. Louis, Columbia University School of the Arts, and The College of Wooster: those thrilling workshops and late night discussions, as well as your thoughts and comments on my work, will never be forgotten.

Maison Auriolles, in Bias, France—thank you to Luc de Bernis and everyone. Special thanks to Anthony Vial for reading *Ghost Letters*, Aurélia Zahedi, for the loyalty, joy and honest friendship you give, and Chantal Morel, Héloïse Zahedi, Marie Rue, Thomas Perrot, and last but not least, Christophe Armand.

Finally, I also would kindly like to thank Washington University in St. Louis and its Chancellor Fellowships program. Without it, my creative time and goals would have been difficult to manage. To the comparative literature program, African and African-American studies, all my professors and mentors, and my students—gratifying credits to you all.

A Glossary: Notes on *Ghost Letters*

Page 5

Bilay wallah is Arabic and means *I swear to God.*

The quotation comes from the Martinican cultural theorist Frantz Fanon's *Black Skin White Masks* (1967) originally published in 1952. Fanon inspired me to open the book this way because of his letters (letters he wrote to his mother, when he was in Algeria).

Surah or *Sūrat* is Arabic, a unit in the Koran or Qur'an.

Sūrat al Balad is the 90th verse of the Koran.

Sūrat al Falaq is the 113th verse of the Koran.

Mukhtâr is the village chief.

Sūrat al Fātihah is the first verse of the Koran.

The *Baobab* tree is important in Senegalese culture. It is a very important symbol in *Ghost Letters* (it comes up for sacred reasons and rootedness).

Casamance is the southern coast of Senegalese.

Bougeureub is a *Diola* dance, from the *Fogny Diolas* tribe in Casamance. I am partly *Diola fogny.*

Bougeureub is usually a dance during marriage celebrations and village rituals.

Bougeureub is composed of one drummer with 4 drums and he is the only performer who does not dance among the crowd that take turn to dance.

Page 8

Suma tour ak suma khél ak jeekeen baléeh—my name and my heart or conscience and that other woman.

The quotation toward the end of this poem is from Elizabeth Alexander's article "The Trayvon Generation" published in *The New Yorker*, June 22, 2020. I was inspired by the voice, so I decided to turn it into a Ghost Mother.

Page 10

The title of this poem is modified. It was first titled Sibeth Fatouma Yalla Mame Ndiaye, which is a Senegalese name. The poem was inspired by Sibeth Ndiaye, who is Senegalese-French. She has been the communication consultant and spokeswoman for President Emmanuel Macro since April 2019. She drew attention in France because she was black, and I see her as a very powerful woman who will inspire so many generations to come.

Nasaraane bou méy jangeu dafa doy seuck?—The English or French or any western language I am learning is enough or is done.

Damaiy déem Senegal—I'll be going to Senegal.

Bignona is a city on the southern coast of Senegal.

Page 12

This poem was inspired by a family photograph in which all their faces are stripped away and the rest of the photo seemed useless, so I decided to write a poem in response to the damaged photo.

Page 13

The line "A bone in the bridge of my throat is permanently out of place" was inspired by a historic event in the Lynching of Laura and L.D. Nelson on May 25, 1911. I did not want to rewrite this story, but this line gave me some kind of force to recreate a narrative.

Bunta safara lay dém ak sama basang—Heading to the gates of Hell with my prayer rug.

Dama beugueu ndéki ak askane bï sene yark tass—I want to have breakfast with the disappointed poor people.

Xalam or *Khalam* is a traditional West African music instrument.

Tama is a talking drum and is used in Senegalese music.

Page 15

Bissap is hibiscus juice in *Wolof*

Page 16

Jaam nga fanan khamo lou sama mame guiss—Did you sleep well? You don't know what my ancestors went through.

A reference to slavery, I was thinking that no matter how much I write about slavery I will never understand the level of suffering they went through. But my roots contain some threads of the Black diaspora and the story I am trying to trace in this poem.

Gnoune gneup ay badolé légnou gnon gnii kii ni di beukeu dée ak hiifeu—We are all poor, and we are dying of hunger.

Page 20

This poem was inspired by the freelance journalist and writer April Zhu based in Nairobi, Kenya. April Zhu's article "A Lost 'Little Africa': How China, Too, Blames Foreigners for the Virus" (2020). Zhu's piece is powerful, and its poeticized dialogue of the black diaspora drew me to the piece. Her piece moved me, so I thought as a dedication I should use her words in this poem. All quotes in this poem are April Zhu's words.

El Dorado—damalén jéppii— I despised rich Western nations.

Abaal ma ghén yayboy deumeuyii damalén diakhaal.—Give or lend me a dream mother I want to baffled these evil people.

Meuneulogno touss deeygney bëett seey frontiéere.—You can't stop Us we will pierce your borders.

Ndax dégg nga Americain?—Do you speak American or Do you speak like an American or Are you American?

Ndax dégg nga nasarran— Can you speak or do you speak English or French or any western language?

Yassa: is a Senegalese dish with fried fish or chicken and lots of onions and white rice.

Page 24

Louy ndéyou talibé booy dem dii yélowan ak yérem you xotékou.—Why the hell do children go begging with ragged clothes?

Bukki di léy deuguë balla guay jaaru ask deumeuyii—Hyena stepping on you before you keep warm with the devils.

Page 27

Fatéwoumala—I did not forget you Ghost Mother.

Santa sama yayboy—Blessing for Mother (in this case), Blessing for Ghost Mother.

Page 29

Youssou N'Dour—Senegalese singer, composer, businessman, politician, and songwriter.

Sougnou Mamboy.— Our grandmother (here referring to Aline Sitoe Diatta) who fought the French when she was twenty-years old. Before Independence in Senegal (1960). History said, she was the first woman to rebuff France's colonial rule in West Africa during colonialization. She is from the *Diola* or *Jola* tribe in Casamance. One of my many tribes.

Page 30

Hamdoulilah is Arabic and means "Thank God!"

Damay dem Senegal sunu gaal—I am going to Senegal our boat.

Sougnou Mamboy—Our grandmother.

Page 33

Dougnou ak jam dougnou ak mbamyii dougnou ack xajjii— enter in peace, enter with pics, enter with the dogs.

Sūrat al Masad— is the 111th verse of the Koran.

Page 35

The last line of this poem called "Fragment" is from Lucille Clifton's poem "God send easter."

Page 36

Walla.—it can also mean "I swear to God" in Arabic.

The quote at the end of this poem is from the Argentinian author Uki Goñi's article "Argentina cordons off virus-hit slum as critics decry ghettoes for poor people" published in *The Guardian* on Wednesday, May 27, 2020. The entire quote is "Valeria Mansilla, a 35-year-old mother of two who lives in Villa Azul, told TN television: 'Tuesday was a terrible day – very stressful – because they brought water and bottled gas [for heating] but only for part of the neighborhood. They brought us powdered milk but we don't have water.'"

Page 39

SSN number—Social Security Number.

Page 41

Seynii weexay nii guy boudoul mëgnii—Their whiteness is like a baobab that does not yield fruits.

The quote at the end of this poem is from Luke Mogelson's article "The Heart of the Uprising in Minneapolis" published in *The New Yorker*, June 22, 2020. I was inspired by Mogelson's ways of relating with all the people he was talking to in this piece. But I also thought that the voice in this piece was brutally honest.

Page 43

Kumpo mask is from Casamance region in Senegal from the *Jola* tribe. The person wearing to Kumpo mask becomes a respected person in the village. Not everyone in the village knows who this person is, but a few elders of the village. The person wearing the Kumpo mask is almost like a myth, and a protector of the village.

Page 44

Yëesu.—Jesus in Wolof

Soo leinn xamoul boulein whxaa ay waxou votée doo tooch doo dara yaafouss—If you don't know or have no idea, do not talk about voting, you are nothing, you are nothing, you are a fraud.

Axëe ack yélefou bagane—Bad deeds and human life, in the sense: referring to a prisoner who has been sentenced for weeks, months, and years, and have no judge or a lawyer.

Ana sama juge—Where is my judge?

Maison d'Arrêt de Reubeuss—The Jail house in Dakar

Maison d'Arrêt de Reubeus: chambre, 40—The Jail house in Dakar; room or cell number 40.

Page 46

This poem went through many revisions and in trying to shape it so that it is relevant to the Ghost Mother figure, I thought about the Ghost Mother's blessing of the dead. I decided in the end that the poem should be an homage to both Freddie Gray and George Floyd.

Page 48

This poem is an homage that speaks about violence. In metaphorized terms, memorize the violent death of Sandra Bland, Micheal Brown, Eric Garner, Freddie Gray, Tamir Rice, and Walter Scott.

Théo Luhaka is referenced to retrace history "Affaire Théo" in France, on Thursday, February 2, 2017 at 4pm four police officers arrested Théo in Rose-des-Vents, at Aulnay-sous-Bois, in the banlieue of Seine-Sain-Denis. From this arrest, Théo is wounded in the anal canal and a section of his sphincter muscle brutalized; he was unable to walk for sixty days.

This "Théo Affaire" is comparable to the Haitian security guard Abner Louima, who was beaten, dehumanized, and abused in 1997 by New York City police officers. The takeaway is that they are both black, and their blackness illustrates violence across the Atlantic: one in New York City and the other not far from Paris (both cities of immigrants and cultures).

Page 49

Yalla teerë lii monme bookognon yellowan guinar saa gaat do darra ak seey toubab yooo ley nekhaal. Fokheul sa gate. Feukheul sa tate do darra.—God forbit, for this we do not want to beg for a rooster, your ass is nothing with your foreigner that sweet talk you, crack your ass, dust your ass, your ass is nothing.

Maison d'Arrêt de Reubeus: chambre 47—The Jail house in Dakar: room or cell number 47.

Le *Joola*—a boat the capsized on Sepetember 26, 2002, near Karabane island.

While numbers were given to be 2,000 dead bodies, we are not exactly sure whether this is true or not. It is said, this tragedy is the African Titanic. Le *Joola* was a ferry that linked Dakar, the capital of Senegal, and Ziguinchor, the capital of Casamance in the south.

Page 52

Sama teewaay moy dara sën teeway doo dara.—My representation is something. Your representation is nothing.

Yéesu ack Yälla –Jesus and Allah.

New thinking was inspired by Rober Hass's *Praise* (1999) and *What Light Can Do: Essay on Art, Imagination, and the Natural World* (2012).

Page 54

Surah or *Sūrat: Al- Fatihah*—is the first verse of the Koran .

Surah or *Sūrat: Al-Nas*— is the 114th verse of the Koran.

Page 55

Sakhal pééxe aggréseuryii sakhal pééxe deumeuyii sakhal kò khél—destroy the swindlers, destroying devil give it a spirit or give it a mind.

The quotation in the middle of this poem is from Ngugi Wa Thiong'o's essay "Return to the Roots: Language, Culture & Politics in Kenya". (1979; reprinted 1997).

Page 57

This poem was inspired by both Edwidge Danticat and Albert Camus.

Page 58

Jokkoo Yallah ak Yéesu ak Kharryii ak Tabaski ak jakarta—Meeting or conversing with Allah and Jesus and lambs and Tabaski and motorbike man.

Tabaski:—Day of Sacrifice where the lamb is killed to honor Ibrahim or Abraham for following God's command in scarifying his son. Tabaski is a big day worldwide for Muslims.

Oussouye: is a village in Casamance.

Karabane Island or Carabane is an island and village in Casamance, on the southern coast of Senegal where the boat *le Joola* was capsized in 2002, killing almost half of its passengers.

Page 61

Degnmey Jonkal Bignona ak yalla khamna dama ragual kankouranrou Casamance ak deumeuyii nék Dakar—They want to circumcise me and God knows I am afraid of *Kankourang* mask in Casamance and evils that settled in Dakar.

Dakar is the capital of Senegal.

Casamance is on the southern cost of Senegal and is known for its abundant natural resources, its rainy season, and tropical landscapes.

Page 63

Fagarù balla gnùy tasù— Take precautions before we recite Senegalese poetry or sing a song.

Ak Sabar—means "with a drum." The line in translation is Doudou N'Diaye Rose with a drum (alluding to the idea that he is known to be the best drummer in Senegal and father of the Senegalese drum).

Deum yii nawaal sama fiit neema loo ragual da lay gaagnë—the devils took my heart and told me that what you fear hurts you.

Mbalax—Senegalese music.

The village's *Tëgg*—The village's blacksmith. The quoted passage in section two of this poem is from Toni Morrison's *The Bluest Eye*.

Hamdoulilah, gnowleen fëgg, gnowleen sëgg gnowleen mëgg deum yii—Thank God, come on and knock on, come on and bend, come on and knock down evils.

Page 64

Degnmey Jébbal Tabaski gnoume gneupeu gneuw gnou feck-fa harbi mou wowe conk—They are going to bury me during Tabaski, all of them came and found the lamb there dried to its corpses.

Îls de Gorée—The slave seaport in Senegal which was used in 15th to 19th century to transport slaves.

Page 66

The quotation in this poem is from Luke Mogelson's article "The Heart of the Uprising in Minneapolis" published in *The New Yorker*, June 22, 2020. The words are spoken by the Somali-born U.S. congresswoman Ilhan Omar.

Page 67

Fatou Diome, diambaroo Senegal ack Tamam ack xéleum bou saf sap nii kouroussou serigne touba—Fatou Diome is a Senegalese heroine with her talking drum and her sharpest mind like the prayer beads of Cheikh Ahmadou Bamba Mbacke.

Cheikh Ahmadou Bamba Mbacke (1853 – 1927) is a religious figure in Senegal, he was exiled by the French.

Page 69

Ghost Mother said, "*Nêkkinam bä foufä neexul kenn ci gnün!*"—Ghost Mother said, "We don't like the way he or she is living there."

This poem is an homage to James Baldwin. The quoted lines in the last lines of this poem are from Baldwin's *If Beale Street Could Talk*.

Page 71

Ajuuma la tey nit demna wax nit dox bi dof bi wax bi dox na wax na sabar dëgg tee xelal niit—Friday it is today human being tell, the work, the foolish, the talk worked, I talked for drum talking for the human being to them good spirit.

Al-Mu'minoon— 118th verse of the Koran.

Al-Qalam—52nd verse of the Koran.

Yay boy.—Mother.

Page 73

Ceebu jënn—Senegalese national dish, red rice and fish.

ack— and

Thiakry—Senegalese dessert made of a creamy sweet or mix of yogurt. It is made of millet, which is an essential grain in Senegal.

The quote at the end of the second paragraph of this poem is from Elizabeth Alexander's article "The Trayvon Generation" published in *The New Yorker*, June 22, 2020. I was not able to resist the ending of the voice that I decided to turn into a Ghost Momma.

Nafilas is the last prayer of the night practiced every day during the entire month of Ramadan, and it changes every night from the beginning to the end of Ramadan.

Page 74

Bissap—hibiscus juice.

Bouye—baobab fruit juice.

Page 75

Dem démeuti góor wala baadolo jaamou Wolof bou saf sap jaam booy toye bounte keureum jaamou Diola boo xamadi, jaamou Peul, jaamou Socé, jaamou Lowbée, jaamou Sérer, baadolo dou lekkadi lekk lekatt—Gone, leaving man or a poor, *Wolof* slave that is beautiful and strong, a slave gets wet in front of its home, a rude *Diola* slave, a *Peul* slave or a *Fula* slave, a *Manding* slave, a *Lawbé Worworbé* slave, a *Serer* slave, a poor does not eat and eat again.

Page 78

Dama gàddu adunaa sama bopp ak sama ndogalou yala. Americain wala toubab loo xam cëe kumpo wala kankourang—I have taken earth on my head and God caused it. What does an American or a foreigner know about *Kumpo*'s mask and *Kankourang*'s mask?

Kankourang—spelled differently, as *Kankoran* or *Kankouran*, is a mask for a ritual celebration of the last day the circumcised have healed and family members gather to celebrate this day in groups. The *Kankourang* dance is called *Diambodong*. It is all for the celebration of the circumcised. It originated from the *Mandingo* or *Mandingues* tribe.

Al- Israa.— is the 111th verse of the Koran.

Page 80

Gnac ka laaj sama xamxam—Refusing to ask my knowledge.

The quotations at the last paragraph in this poem are from Luke Mogelson's article "The Heart of the Uprising in Minneapolis" published in *The New Yorker*, June 22, 2020. The words are spoken by the Somali-born U.S. congresswoman Ilhan Omar.

Page 81

In this poem, the line "Founding fathers spilled blood that will never dry," was inspired by Barack Obama's speech a "A More Perfect Union" on March 18, 2008.

Bayda is a city in Libya

Jaam nga fanan khamo lou saa mameboy guiss—Did you sleep well, you don't know what my ancestors saw.

Page 83

Tchouraï—is a natural incense in Senegalese culture; Tchouraï is burned by Senegalese women to welcome, seduce, attract, charm, lure, their lovers to bed or impress them.

Tchouraï—can be burned to dispel Evil and bad luck, which is the message the lines in this poem suggest.

However, I have witnessed many of my aunts in Senegal, burnt their *Tchouraï*. It is impolite for a child to ask a woman about her *Tchouraï* in Senegalese culture. For example, I can't ask Christiane Mame-Ngoné how her *Tchouraï* is. That would be like asking her what she does in her intimate moments with her husband when she is alone with him in her bedroom.

Senegalese wrestlers also use *Tchouraï* before their contests for blessing and good luck.

Gän bou doxot balay reey deem rootii deerett ack xam xam dem dëe—A visitor that farts before he or she kills must fetch blood and knowledge gone dead.

Page 84

Dima enquête si téléphonebi sama yérem dow! Të-khamouma kagn lay gnibissi kagn lay gnibi Sénégalo—Milkman questioning me over the phone saddened me, and I did not know when I was going to return to Senegal.

Page 87

The quote toward the end of this poem is from Charles M. Blow's article "Destructive Power of Despair" appeared in print on June 1, 2020, in the *New York Times*. Mr. Blow has been inspiring to me in terms of his voice and his writing.

References

Alexander, Elizabeth. "The Trayvon Generation." *The New Yorker*, 22 June 2020, www.newyorker.com/magazine/2020/06/22/the-trayvon-generation.

Baldwin, James. *If Beale Street Could Talk*. Penguin UK, 1994.

Clifton, Lucille. *An Ordinary Woman*. Random House,1974.

Fanon, Frantz. *Black Skin, White Masks*. Grove P, 2008.

Goñi, Uki. "Argentina Cordons off Virus-hit Slum Aa Critics Decry 'Ghettoes for Poor People.'" *The Guardian*, 1 July 2020, www.theguardian.com/world/2020/may/27/argentina-cordons-off-coronavirus-slum-ghettoes-for-poor-people.

Hass, Robert. *Praise*. HarperCollins, 1999.

—. *What Light Can Do: Essays on Art, Imagination, and the Natural World*. HarperCollins, 2012.

Blow, Charles M. "Destructive Power of Despair." *New York Times*. 31 May 2020. www.nytimes.com/2020/05/31/opinion/george-floyd-protests.html.

Mogelson, Luke. "The Heart of the Uprising in Minneapolis." *The New Yorker*, 22 June 2020, www.newyorker.com/magazine/2020/06/22/the-heart-of-the-uprising-in-minneapolis.

Morrison, Toni. *The Bluest Eye*. Random House, 2014

Thiong'o, Ngugi W. *Writers in Politics: Essays*. East African Publishers, 1981.

The Washington Post, 18 Mar 2008, www.washingtonpost.com/wp-dyn/content/article/2008/03/18/AR2008031801081.html?sid=ST2008031801183.

Zhu, April. "A Lost 'Little Africa': How China, Too, Blames Foreigners for the Virus." *The New York Review of Books*, 5 May 2020, www.nybooks.com/daily/2020/05/05/a-lost-little-africa-how-china-too-blames-foreigners-for-the-virus/.

About the Author

Baba Badji is a Senegalese-American poet, translator, researcher, and PhD candidate in Comparative Literature at Washington University in St. Louis. He came to America when he was eleven years-old. He currently lives in St. Louis, but his permanent home is Senegal, where his extended family remains, and New York City. Badji's research and teaching interests center on the links between the various forms of postcolonial studies, theory, and practice, with a particular focus on debates about postcolonial translation theory and Négritude in Anglophone and Francophone cultures. Besides English and French, he is fluent in Wolof, Mending, and Diola, and he calls on these languages in his writing.

Photograph of the author by Sean Garcia.
Used by permission.

Free Verse Editions

Edited by Jon Thompson

Lightning Source UK Ltd.
Milton Keynes UK
UKHW010409240920
370397UK00001B/53